D0038956

Ice:
Tools and Technique

Duane Raleigh

Copyright © 1995 by Elk Mountain Press

All rights reserved. No part of this publication may be reproduced
or transmitted in any form, or by any means without
written permission from the publisher.

Elk Mountain Press
1101 Village Road, Suite LL-1B
Carbondale, CO 81623
(970) 963-9449
First Printing 1995

Library of Congress Catalog Card Number: 95-61190

Raleigh, Duane 1960-
Ice: Tools and Technique

Illustrated by Mike Clelland
Book design by R. Given Jones
ISBN 1-887216-00-6

Printed in the United States of America

10 9 8 7 6 5 4 3 2 1

Most of the activities depicted herein carry a significant risk of personal injury or death. Rock
climbing, ice climbing, mountaineering, and other outdoor activities are inherently dangerous. The
owners, staff and management of CLIMBING MAGAZINE do not recommend that anyone participate
in these activities unless they are experts, seek qualified professional instruction and/or guidance,
are knowledgeable about the risks involved, and are willing to personally assume all responsibility
associated with those risks.

TABLE OF CONTENTS

Water ice in Rifle, Colorado.

Why climb ice?

Roy was halfway up the Lee Vining icefall when the storm slammed into us. My jacket froze into sheet metal, and my toes went so cold you could have snapped them off and shot marbles with them. Then the wind picked up and all I could see was the rope disappearing into the mad white.

Hours passed. The rope fed out in the smallest increments. What was Roy doing up there? What was I doing here? My rough, impatient tongue was on fire. It was my first time on steep ice, and I had only come along because someone had said this ice outside Mammoth Lakes, California, would be a great initiation. It was.

An occasional cry like that of a kicked animal rode the wind. Did Roy want slack? Tension? Was he falling? I felt the rope trying to gauge what was happening, much as a fly fisherman feels the line to detect a strike. Nothing.

I waited. I guessed it was about 8 p.m. Late, and the storm wasn't about to slacken. Screw ice climbing, I thought, as I began to worry about getting my bald-tired VW Bug out the snow drifted road.

The rope quit moving. I tromped around trying to stay warm until I was in a hole up to my knees. Was ice climbing always this miserable?

"I'm going," I told myself, and started climbing. The rope hung in a limp loop, then snapped up tight. Roy must be on top. Or else we were simulclimbing. Who knew? You do what you do and hope it's right.

It wasn't too bad. But ice is always that way when the rope is slapping you in the face. Roy had done us proud: the screws were a healthy distance apart down low. Higher, though, they were only a body-length apart, the sure sign of an epic. What had happened?

I pulled up to the belay in the dark. "My hands are frozen," were Roy's first words. He displayed a set of frosty, blue claws.

"Yah, moine r hoo, hess het out ah heer," I said, and touched my face. It felt like wood.

We postholed down around the cliff's right side and wallowed out through the squeaky snow. My road fears were confirmed — several times the Volkswagen slid sideways, nearly putting us in the creek.

The next day I learned that Roy's hands really were frozen, unlike mine, which had just been cold. Big, taut, water-balloon blisters welled up on his fingers. How could skin stretch so much?

Roy's hands were ruined. His rotting fingers couldn't shovel snow or do any of the other odd jobs we'd hired on at the lodge to do. He would have to leave and convalesce elsewhere. I watched him drive away in his old camper-shell truck, steering with his palms.

Me, I was hooked. Just the thought of ice was a tumbler of white sugar to my blood. It came to a head that same winter when I got fired from my maintenance job for sneaking out midday and trying, with Walt Shipley, to climb the thin, white ribbon that slashed down from the valley rim across from the lodge. We didn't make it, and got fired for being slackers, but I had no regrets, and even now, over a decade later, I shiver with anticipation every time I pick up the axes.

Ice climbing is like that. You love it. You hate it. You feel the pain and revel in the ecstasy — often simultaneously. Ice is a monster with many claws that will gouge out the truth about yourself. You learn more in a dripping, fearful 10 feet of ice than in a century of key tapping or nail pounding or whatever it is you do for a living.

Be warned: Ice is addictive. Front-point to the top of a snow-swept peak or a pillar of plastic, blue ice and you'll forever crave the sweetness. You'll do whatever it takes to sneak off to the mountains and poke around in the cold. And, when you return — back bent, face burned and peeling, knuckles bruised and swollen — you'll be laughing like a loon.

I awoke from The Sickness at the age of 45,

calm and sane, and in reasonably good health

except for a weakened liver and the look

of borrowed flesh common to all who survive

The Sickness.

William S. Burroughs, *The Naked Lunch*

Duncan Ferguson cutting loose in Rocky Mountain National Park.

2 TOOLS

Tools

The meandering creeks that saw into Tulsa's brushy lime-
stone outcrops and feed the muddy Arkansas River don't
freeze often, but when they do, they beckon like dirty maga-
zines to a youth. One bitter winter day, a local boulderer
couldn't stand it any more. He unbolted the kickstand from
his bicycle, and, using it as an ice dagger — he didn't own a
real ice axe — hacked his way up the first ascent of
Chandler Falls.

The climb was, I'm sure, deeply satisfying, with those
moments of baleful regret that signal real adventure.
Moments most of us can find aplenty with the proper tools.

Ice climbing is equipment dependent — much more so
than rock climbing. On rock, you can climb with bare feet
and hands if you must. Try the same on ice and see how far
you get. Tools are your sole link to the ice, and the quality of
those tools will, in part, dictate how well you climb ice — so
buy good ones. Don't get the dregs out of a shop's clearance
bin, and don't settle for your buddy's second-hand antiques.
Max out that credit card. When you're up there with spindrift blasting your neck like electricity, debt will be the least
of your worries. You wouldn't buy a second-hand pacemak-
er, would you?

Piolet with tied leash

Importance of proper selection

The ice axe is to an ice climber and mountaineer what the hammer is to a carpenter. As any carpenter knows, hammers come in many designs and weights, each suited to a specific job, and matching the tool to the task is necessary for quality work. For instance, use a roofing hatchet to nail on a length of delicate base trim and you'll bend the nail and splinter the wood. Similarly, you'll have problems taking a mountaineer's piolet (pee-o-lay) to a frozen waterspout, or tackling snowed-up mountain slopes with a short, technical tool.

The piolet

The piolet is the mountaineer's axe. A proper one has a steel head, aluminum being too soft to suffer the abuse you'll administer to it. The *alpine* pick, the one you want with this sort of tool, has a sickle's curve with deep teeth running the full length.

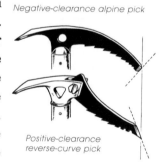

Negative-clearance alpine pick

The end of the pick can have either positive or negative clearance (see illustration). A negative-clearance pick works best for self-arresting, one of the vital functions of this type axe.

Opposite the pick is the adze, the flat, cutting blade you use to gouge

Positive-clearance reverse-curve pick

out your eyes, chop occasional steps, bollards, and rest shelves, carve out cramped bivy platforms, and scour away loose and rotten snow and ice. Between the pick and adze is a hole. This is for threading a wrist leash, but check it to see that it will also accept a carabiner; there will be times when you'll need to clip directly to the head.

The shaft should be either naked or lightly covered with an insulating grip. Shun thick, rubber-coated shafts, which make the tools hard to plunge into packed snow. For that same reason, the spike on the end of the shaft should be simple and dagger pointed.

Get a 65- to 75-centimeter piolet. Go too short and you'll climb hunched over, mopping sweat off your brow in an inef-

ficient and unbecoming pose. Too long and the tool will swing awkwardly. The best length depends on your height and the steepness and type of climbs you'll tackle most often. Shorter climbers will, naturally, benefit from a shorter axe, and taller climbers will need a longer axe. Usually. On steep slopes (steep is subject to individual interpretation, but any slope over 60 degrees can be considered steep), the uphill hand, which always carries the axe, will be close to the snow, making a shorter axe preferred. Low-angle slopes require a longer axe, as does sugary snow, where a short axe makes a sketchy shaft belay.

The axe should balance well, comfortably fit your hand, and have a light yet solid feel. A flimsy tool is too bouncy

The piolet is your support and self-belay on moderate snow and ice.

and feels squirrely, undermining your confidence. Knock a tool hard against your boot sole to check its sturdiness. If it vibrates like a tuning fork, shelve it.

No piolet is complete without a leash. Pick one that opens and closes securely and easily, even when you're wearing mittens, and is runner strength. Get a leash that you tie through the axe head and is slightly longer than the axe shaft. Or make your own by tying a strap of 1/2-inch webbing through the head, hitching it once around the shaft, and finishing it with a generous wrist loop, which you can twist to tighten.

Water-ice tools

The tools you need for steep water ice are radically different from those you use in the snowy mountains. For starters, technical, waterfall-type ice demands *two* tools: an axe, similar to but shorter than the piolet, and a hammer. It is tempting to get an axe from one company and a hammer from

Kevin "Bones" Cooney sampling tricky Quebec ice.

6 TOOLS

another. Stick with one brand. That way, both tools will swing alike and, in the case of modular tools, they'll use the same picks and wrenches.

Once you start leading, you really need three tools. The third tool you keep holstered at the ready and use as a backup in case a main tool breaks or you drop one. Many climbers use a shorter, hammer-headed version of their main tools. Others choose a different model, thus extending their tool selection.

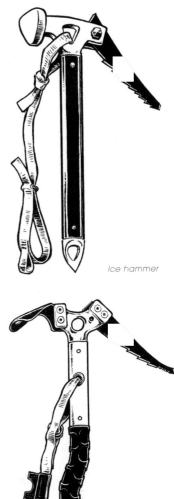

Ice hammer

The technical axe has an adze like the piolet. Many also have an optional spade-like adze that you can use as a "pick" in soft ice and hard snow, where the real pick would shear through. This adze shape is also useful for twisting and camming in rock or ice cracks. Starting out, you'll rarely use an adze this way. Remember that an adze's primary job is chopping, and select it for that function first.

Hammer heads look and work as you'd think — for pounding. Some are round, others square, and still others have a hex or wedge shape that you can jam in tapering cracks.

Piolets usually have a solid, one-piece head, but technical tools are nearly always modular, a design that lets you replace broken picks or switch pick designs to accommodate varying ice

Bent-shaft tool

conditions. Although more expensive than solid-head tools, modular tools are nearly essential for serious waterfall ice.

Select a modular tool that isn't going to rattle loose or require more than a wrench or two to change picks. The best designs use a tongue-and-groove fit to position the pick, and are machined so close that you have to use gentle force to press the pick into its slot.

Steep ice calls for short tools. Fifty centimeters is about right, but five centimeters either way is still on the money.

Short tools offer dexterity and are easier to pound and chop with, especially in tight spots like chimneys. The greater reach of longer tools gets you up a stretch of ice with fewer placements, and lets you avoid some rotten placements you'd be forced into using with shorter tools.

Curved shaft or straight? Curved-shaft proponents say these protect your knuckles from smashing more than straight shafts. Truth is, when you're starting out you're going to mash those knuckles like potatoes, bent shaft or no. What bent shafts really do is give you more shaft clearance for hooking over bulges and cauliflowers. And, because the bend keeps your fingers from getting pinned against the ice, your hands stay warmer. For those reasons, most waterfall ice enthusiasts prefer bent shafts, while alpine climbers prefer straight shafts, which work better for plunging in snow.

Don't worry too much about shaft design; you'll get used to whatever you use. Do concern yourself with the picks. Get a *reverse-curve* pick for each tool. Reverse-curve picks are the best for "hooking" rotten and chandeliered ice. If you are going into the mountains, switch out the reverse-curve with an alpine or Alaskan pick, which, because of their gentler curves, are better for self-arresting.

Either pick should have a full row of piranha teeth extending from the end of the pick to its juncture with the head. The teeth near the tip should be fine and relatively shallow so they are solid in thin ice yet easy to clean. Teeth near the shaft should get more aggressive, for hooking large features such as cauliflowers. Most picks have a good set of teeth, but if yours are lacking you can use a round metal file to cut additional ones, or to modify the existing ones.

Keeping a firm grip on your tool is crucial for precise placements. Slick shafts spin and turn cockeyed when you swing. Manufacturers know this, so nearly all ice-tool shafts come dipped or wrapped in rubber.

You say you've found the ideal tools? Let's check. Pick one up. Bang the flat of its head sharply on a hard floor. How did it feel? Did it vibrate? It shouldn't. A good ice tool will absorb the shock in its head and shaft. You can bang it against a rock and feel nary a tremor at your hand. It should feel SOLID. The tool should swing like a 28-ounce Stanley framing hammer, with most of the weight in the head, and have a shaft that you can easily clamp your gloved or mitted fingers around. Shaft diameter won't be a problem if you have large hands, but people with petite hands should seek a skinny, easy-to-wrap handle — fat ones will be too pumpy.

A good wrist loop locks you to your tool like a bull-rider's thong.

Wrist loops

Matching the tool to the task and your physique is important, but a bad wrist loop will make even the best tools feel clumsy. Wrist loops that don't stay cinched will force you to overgrip and flame out, leading to a sloppy swing and poor tool plants. A good wrist loop is simple, runner strength, and locks you in tight. Like a bull-rider's thong, it puts the load on your wrist, letting you maintain a light yet secure grip. There are a lot of wrist loops out there, but only a few really work.

Attach the wrist loops to your tools so your *mitted* claws rest just above the spike. A common mistake is to cut the loops too short, causing you to constantly choke up on the shafts, shortening your reach, and compromising your swing. When in doubt, make the loops too long — you can always put a couple twists in them to shorten them.

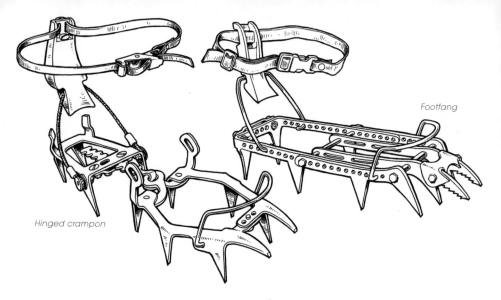

Hinged crampon

Footfang

Crampons

Competent ice climbing means mastering balance, just as in rock climbing. Sure, you have ice tools, and when the angle is steep you pull on them as freely as you do on a fingerboard, but depend on them too much and you'll waste energy. Efficient, graceful ice climbing involves centering your weight over your feet. And precise footwork mandates good crampons.

Crampons come in two designs: hinged (or flexible) and rigid. Hinged crampons are built so they flex just behind the ball of the foot, making them easy to walk in when paired with an equally flexible boot.

Hinged crampons are ideal for mountaineering, where you mostly crampon flat foot on low-angle ice. They also work for front-pointing steep ice, though for the latter use you must mate them to a perfectly rigid boot. Match a flexible crampon to a flexible boot and you may as well front-point in flip-flops.

Vertical front point

For steep ice buy rigid crampons. These are solid and generally more precise than hinged crampons. But, like hinged crampons, rigid crampons aren't great for everything. They are awkward to walk in and love to ball up

Horizontal front point

with snow. The lesson is, match the crampon frame to the job: rigid for pillars and steep technical terrain; hinged for moderate mountaineering.

Get the right frame, then examine the front points. These can be either horizontal or vertical. Either type is fine once you get used to them, but the broad horizontal points hold best in snow and soft ice, like the stuff you find on most mountains, thus these points are common on hinged crampons. Technical water-ice crampons typically have vertically oriented front points, serrated steak knives that slice into hard and brittle ice cleanly and with minimal effort.

Crampon bindings

My first crampons were state-of-the-art, Chouinard, 12-point rigids, fully adjustable, and decked out with Beck neoprene straps and nickel buckles. They served me well 15 years ago and would do the same today if I were to get nostalgic and root them out of the shed. I doubt I ever will. Strap-on crampons are out. Step-ins are in.

Step-in crampon bindings work much like randonee ski bindings. A metal bail fits into the boot's toe welt, and a rear lever snaps over the heel welt, tensioning the toe bail.

Match the toe bail to the shape of your boot. Some bails are squared, others oval. A square bail on an oval-toed boot is an accident waiting to happen, as is an oval bail on a square-toed boot. Fit square to square and oval to oval. Also, match the heel bail so it snaps up cleanly and holds firm to your boot.

Boots

Keep your feet warm and dry and you might actually enjoy yourself. Plastic double boots are first choice, being waterproof, stiff for front-pointing, and toasty warm. However, don't abandon leather boots altogether. For warm, near-freezing conditions, leather boots that are compatible with step-in crampons — sufficiently stiff and grooved for bails —

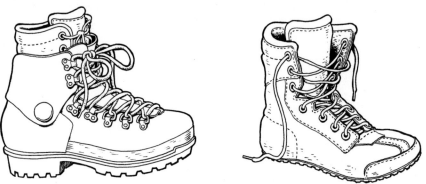

Double boot with liner boot

are ideal. Their lower bulk and lighter weight gives you a more sensitive feel for the ice, and you can even climb moderate rock in them. Ideally, you'll have a pair of each type boot.

Examine the toe and heel grooves on all boots. The grooves must be deep enough to securely hold the crampon bails. To double-check this, snap your crampons on the boot. Deep grooves that swallow the bails are what you want. While you have the crampons on the boot, check the Achilles' area to see that it is firm. A mushy heel counter will let the crampon's heel lever bite into your Achilles' tendon.

Almost all plastic and leather boots are stiff, but, like whiskey, some are stiffer than others. What you get hangs on what you will use the boots for most. Gully climbers and mountaineers, who need boots that walk better than they front-point, should select a model with semi-pliable uppers. These are less fatiguing to sneak around in, are better at flat-foot cramponing, and are more comfortable than rigid boots. Technical ice climbers will benefit from boots with rigid uppers that lock the feet into solid front-point mode regardless of how much you shake and quiver.

Any boot should fit close without squeezing your feet. Try on the boots when you're wearing a thin liner and heavy outer sock, the same socks you'd climb in. A slightly loose fit is better than tight. Pay close attention to the forefoot. Boots that squeeze the ball of your foot are too small and will compromise blood circulation to the toes. Fit the toe perfectly — if, after that, your heel lifts, shim the heel with L-pads (available at ski shops) to snug it up. Plastic boots don't stretch (the liners will compress some, eventually giving you slightly more room) so how they fit in the shop is how they are going to fit years ahead. Take your time and get it right.

Handwear

I've never seen anyone rock climb in flip-flops, but I have watched hordes of ice climbers handicap themselves with leaky, stiff, or slick mittens and gloves. Select your handwear more carefully than your beer.

Lobster mitts

Gloves or mittens? Mittens are nearly always warmer and, contrary to what many climbers think, aren't necessarily more cumbersome than gloves. Thin, pliable mittens, for instance, give you better dexterity than overinsulated, stiff gloves.

On warmish, wet, early and late-season ice, a good combination is thick poly-pro gloves worn inside a *seam-taped, waterproof* mitt or glove shell that has a rubberized palm and a long gauntlet that you can cinch down with your teeth.

When that combo isn't warm enough, switch to an insulated mitten; the "lobster" type with separate index fingers are useful for twisting in screws and clipping carabiners. As a backup, carry a spare pair of gloves in the chest pocket of your bibs, and have a cozy, warm pair of mittens, like the wool Dachsteins, handy for belaying.

Selecting handwear is a huggermugger, and after going through a dozen different types, I haven't found the perfect setup. I do, however, know what not to get. Avoid anything made of leather, anything with down insulation, and anything made for downhill skiing. Also avoid shells with unsealed seams, which you can seal yourself, but will still leak.

Harnesses

You can use your crag harness for ice climbing, but unless you bought it when you were 50 pounds heavier or it adjusts,

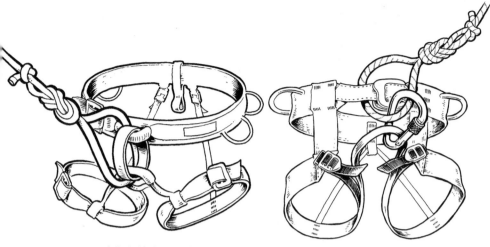

Adjustable harness   Diaper harness

it isn't going to fit over the winter clothing you'll be wearing. As with all useful items, an ice climbing harness must be simple. Padding isn't necessary and absorbs water. A fully adjustable harness made for ice climbing is best. Get one with a couple of gear loops and a belay/rappel loop.

One popular ice climbing harness is the "diaper," which has a crotch loop in lieu of leg loops. Clipping this loop to the waist belt with a locking carabiner (instead of tying the rope through it, as you'd do rock climbing) lets you drop the loop to answer nature's call and remove bottom layers without messing with the rope, which remains tied through the harness waist belt. The diaper is less comfortable, however, and its lack of a belay/rappel loop complicates rope management.

Helmets

Do you want to live? Then wear a helmet, not so much to protect your noggin in a fall, but to shield it from the debris that storms down ice and mountain routes. A helmet won't save you from the ice-chest-sized chunks, but it will protect you from the smaller pieces that can still kill or cause you to fall. The many gouges in any ice climber's helmet will attest to its usefulness.

Select a helmet that doesn't interfere with your visibility or movement, and has retainer straps for holding a headlamp.

Ropes

You'll need two ropes for most ice and alpine climbs, which typically require one or many double-rope rappels to get back down. Get either two 9mm ropes and lead using the double-rope technique, or pair a 10mm with a 8- or 9mm rope, and lead on the 10mm by itself, same as you would on rock, and pair it with the smaller rope for the rappels.

Your rope is going to get dripped on, chucked in puddles, and dragged through wet snow, making a strong argument for a rope with a water-repellent coating. Don't expect a miracle from "dry" ropes, though. Treated ropes still get wet and freeze; they just do it slower than untreated ones. Help yourself by getting a treated rope, then retire it to rock climbing once it starts fuzzing up — ratty, old ropes soak up the juice like sots.

The fashionable Brit Phil Thornhill on the approach to the Grand Jorasses, Chamonix, France.

Rope length is up to you. Fifty-meter ropes are standard, but 55-meter or 60-meter ropes let you skip occasional belay stances and get down with fewer rappels. Better all the way around.

Let your legs do the work. Duncan Ferguson on his home turf – Colorado ice.

Moving

To climb ice and snow is to dance on butcher knives. Intoxicating, and, if you misstep, dangerous. It is a dance where the time and steps change constantly with the condition of the ice and its steepness. Yet that does not make it difficult or complicated. The basic moves are few and simple: You swing and step, and you swing and kick. Learning the motions and knowing when to use them takes a bit of schooling, and then it's practice, practice, practice.

Getting comfortable

You dream of leading vertical sheets of rotten, unprotectable ice and endless ramparts of snow, but the reality is you'll need to spend several seasons getting your sea legs by following an experienced partner. Augment that with as many days of ice bouldering and toproping as you can squeeze in. The bouldering is especially important. A couple of days close to the ground will teach you more about movement and technique than a season of moaning around on a rope.

Seek out a 40- to 50-degree flow and evaluate it for safe bouldering. What will happen should you take an unroped spill? Will you slide into jagged ice blocks? The highway? Unless the landing is ideal — deep, soft snow — go elsewhere. Even when the landing is good, try not to fall. Those short, body-length falls you're accustomed to taking in rock shoes are enough to snap an ankle or wrist if a crampon or tool snags the ice. When in doubt, or if the cliff is a bit too high or the descent precarious, use a toprope.

Good ice climbers move deliberately. They set their tools and crampons with a minimum of whacks and negotiate the ice with a sure grace, much like a practiced rock climber who seemingly drifts up a steep face. Though good ice and rock climbers are working on different mediums, they share a common trait: Both are comfortable.

You get comfortable by first getting confident. And you get confident by practicing. To start, get a feel for your boots, crampons, and tools, and for moving in heavy clothes and mittens. Forget about climbing; simply get dressed, snap on the crampons, and walk around in the snow and ice. Just moving will be challenge enough at first. Your feet will feel big and heavy. Your crampons will catch on your pant legs. Your clothes will feel like armor.

You'll find that it helps to walk with your feet slightly apart and lifted higher than normal to clear the crampon points. Don't worry if you feel uncoordinated. Everything is new and will take getting used to. Keep kicking around, then walk up the lowest angle bumps. Carry the tools by the head, pick facing away from you. Don't swing them yet, just get used to holding them.

Test the adhesion of your crampons by "frictioning" around, much as you did with your rock shoes when you were learning to rock climb. Try lightly stepping. How did they hold? Then set them harder. Is that better? Now stomp them in.

Walk up the slope. Walk down it. Sidestep up it and side-step down it. Zig-zag. Stomp up the slope backward, then back down it. Don't just set your crampons anywhere. Pick a spot and watch your foot go onto it, just as you'd set a rock shoe on a hold.

Clomp around until you feel like you were born with those points on your feet. Now let's work with your tools.

The swing

Find a near-vertical wall. Walk up to it, but, again, forget about climbing. With both feet on the ground, practice planting and removing the tools. Keep a light yet firm grip on the shafts. Fight the urge to overgrip, but don't get so lackadaisical that the tool spins and hits the ice crookedly.

Swing your tools with thought and precision. Find the "sweet spot" in the ice, those places where the pick will glide in with minimal fracturing or effort. Experience will give you an eye for these places — divots, creases between

Mark a spot and hit it

icicles, and smooth, gummy-looking areas. Mark your spot with an imaginary X, and whack it with the same accuracy you'd use to drive a nail.

Hit the ice with the pick, not your knuckles. With some tools you swing by pulling the pick down and into the ice, like you're plunging a dagger into your enemy's chest. Others require a subtle wrist flick and still others take a natural arc, karate-chop style. Find out what works best with your tools and strive for a solid stick with one stroke. Beginners tend to hack until all the blood is in their arms instead of their brains. Focus. Use sure, swift strokes. All that chopping will only tire you out and destroy the placement, especially when the ice is brittle or thin.

Once you get reasonably comfortable with the basic plant, experiment with your tools. Set them shallow. Do they still hold? Now bury them to the hilt. Efficient ice climbing depends on finding that fine line where the tools are solid but still clean easily. Overdrive your tools and you'll get pumped and frustrated trying to clean them.

Learn to exploit your tools. Take advantage of their strengths, and respect their limits. Find out how much outward pull the tools can take — not much usually. With your feet safely on the ground, stick the tools in and see how far you can lift your wrists before the picks pop free. Avoid a nasty reconstruction bill by keeping your face well clear of the tool, where it will slice nothing but air should it rip.

Pause on each placement and evaluate it. How did it sound? Hollow? Muffled? How did it feel? Did it vibrate? How does it look? Especially watch out for dinner-plating. You'll know when this happens because the ice will fracture with a distinct, unsettling "whump," and an area of ice about the size of a dinner plate or larger will suddenly turn opaque white. When you try to pull up on it, the whole chunk will come off on your head.

Before this happens, gently remove your tool, trying to keep the plate intact. Find a better placement elsewhere or break the plate into smaller pieces and plant your tool in the better ice underneath. Don't move up on a dinner-plate placement or carelessly step on it once you get higher. Either could cause a fall.

Cold, brittle ice and the ice on bulges is prone to dinner-plating, but you can run into this problem anywhere, any time, except in chandeliered and rotten ice, which have their own nightmares, discussed later in The Changing Medium.

Clean a tool by rocking up and down on the shaft. Bump the underside of the adze or hammer head with your palm to knock loose a stuck tool. Avoid removing a stuck tool by torquing it sideways — you'll snap the pick.

Feel comfortable yet? If not, continue swinging. If so, it's time to climb.

French technique

The basic tenet for climbing rock holds true for climbing snow and ice: keep the weight on your feet. On low-angle slopes, those up to 50 degrees or so, set your crampons flat and balance over them. This is French technique.

French technique is simple, yet many climbers ignore it and front-point up everything, even ridiculously low-angle ice. Those climbers are like the bicyclist who refuses to change gears — he gets by but is never efficient.

French technique comes into its own on relentless mountain slopes, but you'll use it on vertical water ice as well. Almost any pillar will have shelves, bumps, or low-angle spots that you can flat-foot with at least one foot, resting that calf by doing so. Neglect the French technique and you'll rob yourself of the ice-climbing equivalent of the kneebar.

The angle and hardness of the ice — and stiffness of your boots — will determine how you place your feet and how many tools you need. You can simply walk up hard, low-angle ice and steeper bits of soft ice. Carry an axe in the uphill hand, walking-stick style, and use it as a balance point, not a crutch. With all French-technique positions, plunge the crampons into the ice with vigor, like you're stomping a bug. Merely placing the crampons as if you're out on a stroll will lead to a sudden refresher in self-arresting.

Once the angle tips up and regular walking is out, splay your feet and continue with the one axe in your uphill hand. When that position is no longer comfortable, sidestep. As with the previous two positions, sidestepping usually requires a single tool. Hold the tool in your dominant hand and plant it ahead of you. Pull on the shaft, palm the slope with your other hand, and advance your feet. Too steep for that and you'll need to get both hands on the axe. Hold the shaft with one hand, and grasp the head with the other. Be

Modified French technique

Sidestepping

careful not to pull out on the axe or let the shaft drop against the ice — both mistakes will dislodge the teeth. Pull straight down on the axe and move your feet up. Get your feet as high as is comfortable and keeps you in balance, then gently remove the axe and stick it higher.

One of the common beginner mistakes is to try to belly crawl up the face. Keep your body away from the wall, where you are in balance and have a clear view of the terrain ahead. Lean in and your feet will shoot out from under you.

Last, when the ice is too steep for sidestepping, front-point with one foot and sidestep with the other. Use two tools and advance them by either alternating with

---

TROUBLE-SHOOTING YOUR SWING

You want your tools to slide into the ice, cleanly, solidly, and with minimal effort. That doesn't always happen, of course, but if it's a rarity, read on. The following are common problems, causes, and preventives.

- Bashing your knuckles. This is caused by a host of ills. Most likely, the arc of your swing isn't compatible with the curve or droop of your picks, or with the bend in your shafts. The solution is simple: Adjust your swing. To do this, concentrate on the very tip of the pick. Don't look at the pick, just get a sense for where it is. Leer at the spot where you want the pick to land, and don't take your dry eyes off of it. Swing in slow motion a couple times to find the right angle, then go full speed. Watch the pick as it impacts the ice, just as you eye a baseball hitting the bat or a tennis ball striking the racket, and the pick, not your knuckles, will strike the ice.

- You bash your knuckles no matter what you do. Check your wrist leashes. They may be too short, or twisted, causing you to grab the shaft too high. Unkink or lengthen your leashes so you grab the shaft just above the spike, where the tool was designed to be gripped.

- You bash your knuckles now and then. You are either getting in a rush, are too tense, or your hands are frozen. Slow down. Take a deep breath and grunt. Thaw your hands by shaking them down by your waist, and buy warmer gloves or mittens at the first opportunity.

- You only bash your knuckles when you swing over bulges. You're not alone; every ice climber does this now and then, usually during lapses into la-la land. Swinging over bulges is tough because the edge of the bulge is closer to you than the spot over the shelf where the pick will strike. Exaggerate your swing so the tool shaft and your hand clear the lip.

your feet, as if you're climbing a ladder, or by planting both tools at the same level, walking both feet up, then replacing the tools higher. In either case, switch foot positions often to equalize the strain.

Front-pointing

Slopes that are too steep or bulletproof for French technique require front-pointing. Do this as you'd think, by kicking the two front points into the face. Before you start, lace your boots tight — slop causes calf pump — and cinch down those wrist loops and helmet strap.

Angle your kick so the front points go slightly down and into the ice and create a steady four-point platform — the two front points and the pair just behind them — to stand on. A common mistake, especially when you tire, is to drop your heels, placing the load on the front points alone, which can then lever out.

Don't kick blindly. Watch your feet and aim for a spot. You

Front-pointing

Make a higher-than-normal arc, then flick the tool down and into the back of the bulge, where the ice is usually the stickiest and least likely to plate away.

■ Pick bounces out. This happens most often on thin ice when your picks go all the way through and hit the underlying rock. You can predict when this is likely much of the time because you can see the shadowy rock under the ice, but when snow blankets the ice you probably won't know it until your tool bounces back at you. The solution? Swing easy. Peck at the ice in micro-swings rather than whale at it.

Letting your picks get worn too short can also cause them to bounce out, as can hitting the ice with the spike or shaft. Replace those nubs and refocus on your swing. Again, glue your eyes to the tip and watch it glide into the ice. Pay close attention when you're slamming the pick into sockets, gouges, and other hollows, where it is easy for the shaft or your knuckles to strike the ice before your pick.

■ Pick glances off. You are probably swinging crookedly or your tools could just be dull. Sharpen the tools and try a firmer grip. Inattention or fatigue can also cause your tools to hit the ice cockeyed, but so can having frozen hands or stiff or slick mittens or gloves. Warm your hands and get pliable gloves or mitts with sticky palms. You'll be surprised how well a simple handwear upgrade will improve your climbing.

■ Ice shatters. Your tools are blunt. Sharpen them. If the tools are sharp and the ice still shatters you are either bashing the dickens out of it, or the ice is just brittle. In both cases, "quiet" your swing to disturb the ice less. Try to get good sticks on the first go. Aim for a sweet spot, hit it, and have faith.

Low heels

are too extended if you can't see your feet. Keep your tools and feet closer together and your chest away from the ice. When you have a small ledge or bump, kick just above it so your side points can settle onto it. The more points in the ice the better. Avoid kicking into icicles. They'll break.

In good, solid ice and hard-packed (neve) snow, set the front points with one or two swift, sure kicks that minimize fracturing and effort. In brittle and thin ice, use short, light kicks, or peck out a little niche and set the points in this. Rotten and chandeliered ice is hardest to work because it breaks away. Sometimes you can gouge little steps by kicking away the rotten surface ice.

Kick straight in so both front points bite equally. Angle your kick and one front point will sink deeper than the other, a precarious situation. I'm bow-legged and have a hard time with this because my feet naturally want to splay. When I get tired and lose concentration, I angle my kicks and my crampons shear out.

How high and how far apart you kick varies according to the angle. On low-angle grades you can kick knee-high and with your feet close together, but as the wall steepens you'll want to shorten your kicks and keep them at shoulder width or wider. Sometimes you won't have a choice. Small-diameter icicles and narrow runnels will force your feet together, or the ice may be so narrow you have to place one foot directly above the other. When that's the case, try not to snag your pants, and move in short steps to keep your balance.

Set the points, then hold your boots steady. Quivering will only vibrate the steel loose, and raising or dropping your heels might disengage the front points. Front-pointing may seem straightforward and easy, but don't get locked into this technique. On steep ice, root out low-angle shelves or bumps that will let you stand flat-footed and give your burning calves a break.

The classic picture of the front-pointer paints her facing the wall, tool in each hand, whacking away. That's correct much of the time, but on transitional slopes, those just too steep for French technique, you might still get by with one tool — fewer tools, fewer swings, less energy spent — using the double-handed axe position you learned earlier. Keep both hands on the axe, or hold the axe in one hand and palm the ice with the other, and pull straight down on it as usual. Face the slope and walk up on your front points. Simple.

Front-pointing with one tool

Use two tools when you no longer feel comfortable or safe with one. Strap a tool to each hand and assume a relaxed, athletic stance, much like the one you learned in Little League. Feet under you at shoulder width, torso slightly bent, arms bent and to the side. Relax. The whole nut to climbing ice is staying loose. Imagine you're watching Lawrence Welk's bubble dancers and flooow.

Avoid short, choppy placements. Be efficient and reach with each tool, but don't extend so far that you lean into the ice. Good placements are nice, but every one needn't be a belay anchor, especially when you're following. One trick you can use to get the most mileage out of your arms is to set one tool high and solid, then lightly place the other beside it. Advance your feet, then remove the less bomber tool and place it high, but now make it the bomber tool. The old bomber tool becomes the lightly set one, and so on.

Whack the tools straight in and land each placement at shoulder width or slightly wider, wherever is best for balance. Swing too far to the side and you'll lose height and

Blending French technique with front-pointing is the most efficient way to climb.

want to barndoor off when you remove a tool to set it higher. Set the picks too close together and the placements can fracture across to each other —a real possibility in brittle or thin ice.

There are two ways to climb ice. You can get mechanical and plow dead ahead, or weave and bop like a rock climber. There are plenty of excellent ice climbers who use either style, or do a bit of both, but until you get a real feel for the ice, you are better off being the machine. Don't do anything fancy; just concentrate on advancing each tool and crampon. Drop knees, stems, and the other elaborate moves will come soon enough.

The cadence goes like this: Set the right tool. Turn your face away from the placement, then test-load it. Apply more weight if it feels good, but keep the main load on your feet. Set the left tool at the same level. Test and load it. Kick in the right crampon at a comfortable height, probably just below the knee. Step up. Place the left crampon at the same height. Remove and reset the right tool higher. Same for the left. Repeat with the crampons.

Moving on snow

The maneuvers that work on ice — front-pointing and French technique — are also the ones you use on snow.

Climbing pure snow, however, requires a few tricks and moves all its own. For starters, you usually use only one tool, the trusty piolet.

Always hold the piolet in your uphill hand, where you can lightly pull on it for balance and catch yourself if your feet slip or the snow breaks out from under them.

Carry the axe with the pick pointed away from you, and plunge the shaft into the snow until you feel confident it has a solid bite. In hard snow, a good spike plant may suffice, but in soft, sugary snow ram the axe to midshaft or even to the hilt.

Advance your feet only after the axe is set. Simply walk on really low-angle snow, advancing the axe every other step, like a cane. Step, stomp, or kick your feet to set them. Snow conditions will tell you what to do, and, dictate whether you need crampons. Your bare boot usually suffices for soft, deep, or wet snow, but when in doubt, it's better to spend a couple of minutes clipping on the crampons than to go pinging down the slope.

Axe walking

Getting snow balled up under your boot soles or crampons is inevitable in wet snow, and it can be dangerous unless you pay attention because the caked-on snow robs you of traction. Banging the side of your crampons or boots with the axe will dislodge the snow; you'll need to do this nearly every step when balling is a problem. Be careful not to nick your axe shaft on a crampon point.

Your feet will naturally splay in French mode according to the angle of the slope. Fine, just make sure your boots are kicked in solidly and you have a good hold on the axe. When the slope is steep enough for you to zig-zag, switch hands so the axe remains in

MAKING ANTI-BALL PLATES

To prevent snow build-up, or balling, on crampons, both rigid and hinged: match-cut a sheet of thick plastic, like the type used for kids' roll-up sleds, to each crampon frame. Take a hot wire and punch holes in each cut-out. Affix them to your crampons with baling wire. Cheap, lacks elegance, but it works well.

the uphill hand. This poses a problem when your hand is cinched in a wrist loop. Discipline yourself to hold the axe with your hand out of the wrist loop. Doing so is faster and less awkward than constantly messing with a wrist loop.

Plotting the course

Picture yourself in Tuolumne Meadows at the base of a fine, orange-striped granite dome. Ahead of you lies 40 feet of undulating handcrack. When you crane your neck, you can see that the crack fades away just as it hooks right. You can also see that the route beyond the crack is covered with nice pinch knobs. How would you climb this pitch? No question. You'd jam the crack, then face climb those warts when it ran out.

In that scenario, you didn't even have to think about what you'd do. The climb told you.

Climb ice the same way. Use whatever technique is logical, and mix it up. Front-point a face that is vertical and smooth, and use French technique combined with front-pointing on rolling ice. Likewise, stem in corners using whatever foot position is most comfortable.

Being new to the game, you'll have to think about which axe and foot positions to use. You'll certainly make mistakes. Don't worry about it. Simply being aware of the game is good enough for now. As you get a couple of seasons under your belt, you'll instinctively switch to the prescribed technique, just as you'd jam the handcrack without giving it a thought.

Bare sheets of strictly front-pointing ice are thankfully rare, though all can appear that way if you get locked into the mindset of pure bashing. Instead, open your eyes and study the ice. You'll find that it's more featured than any rock wall. Over there is a deep ice flute, a gift. Stem or chimney against it. Advance your tools, but try not to load them; keep the weight on your feet. Don't get too extended, or you'll have to "jump" your feet up, a dicey maneuver.

Also, don't get locked into tool-bashing. Sometimes you can drop one or both tools and press against chimney walls, or pinch and layback ribs and icicles. Slip handjams in hollows and in the gaps between icicles.

Most ice climbs have more than one way up them, some more difficult than others. In a couple years you'll be bored with always taking the line of least resistance, and will want to up the ante by attacking the line of strength. For now, though, go the easy route. Weave back and forth on the lower-angle benches, wiggle into chimneys, and stem in corners. Look for the featured sections that will let you stay over your feet.

Picking a path up a snow face is usually straightforward. Go where snow conditions are best and safest — pick the shady half of a face over the sunny side — and where objective dangers are fewest. Don't, for example, expose yourself directly under a cornice or below a band of rotten rock when climbing to one side will get you out of the bomb zone.

Usually, you'll want to zigzag up a snowfield rather than take the straight line. Weaving back and forth, though seemingly slower, saves energy. Use whatever combination of French technique and front-pointing is most efficient. Abandon the basket weave and front-point up the beeline when speed is of the essence, such as when stones are peppering the face, or darkness or storm are fast approaching.

Self-arresting

Walt Shipley and I had completed a route on the North Face of Les Droites, a 5000-foot alpine wall just outside alpine climbing's megacenter, Chamonix, France. Fifty rope-

TAMING THOSE PESKY BULGES

Pulling over a bulge or onto a shelf is one of the trickier moves on ice, and is where many climbers fall. Keeping on your feet is the main problem. With your torso bent over the crest of a bulge you lose sight of your feet and kick blindly. Then, as you advance your tools to the back of the bulge or try to get them in the ice directly above it, you overreach. Your crampons pop, and you're gone.

Avoid this by keeping your tools and crampons closer than normal, and take small, manageable bites. Once you are ready to stand on the ledge, watch that you don't lever out on your tools.

lengths of rock, ice, and bits of both on the drag-on-spine ridge of the Northeast Spur Direct had brought us to the summit ridge by late afternoon.

We spent a drippy night on a cramped ledge on the descent, our thoughts washed

Self-arrest

with anticipation of the hot coffee and fresh bread that awaited us below. After countless rappels, we were glissading, unroped, down a low-angle, crevassed snowslope, the final obstacle between us and the valley floor. Walt, the much better skier, was zooming ahead of me, upright on his feet, holding an axe in an outstretched arm. I slid on my butt sheepishly behind him, afraid that if I stood I'd lose my balance, fall, and be gobbled up by a crevasse. But it wasn't me that went down. I saw a spray of snow arc up. Walt was on his back, zipping straight for a crevasse. "He's a goner," I thought. To my surprise, Walt flipped onto his belly and executed a perfect self-arrest, stopping almost instantaneously.

He got up, slapped the snow from his breeches, and off we went again, Walt still standing resolute, me cowering even lower. It was my first season in the mountains, and I had never seen, let alone practiced, a self-arrest.

My mistake. I vowed never to go out again without being well-versed in this fundamental survival skill. You would do well to do the same. Self-arresting isn't difficult, but it doesn't come naturally, nor does it always work. Fall on even the lowest-angle water ice and you'll zip off to eternity, axe in hand, the pick glancing fruitlessly off the ice. Ditto for hard-packed snow and even steep soft snow. Low-angle snow, the

Belly self-arrest

terrain you're likely to climb or descend unroped, is where the self-arrest can work, though even then it is the court of last resort.

Dedicate an entire afternoon to practicing self-arrests, then follow it up with periodic refreshers. Reaction time is everything. Packed snow has little coefficient of friction. Ice has even less. You accelerate quicker than you'd think. Start sliding and you have only seconds to react.

Practice on a 20- to 30-degree slope with a safe runout — no trees, rocks, cliffs, or highways below. Start with the simplest self-arrest. Grab the head of your piolet (practice with your technical tools later) in your dominant hand, pick away from your body. Brace the axe across your chest by gripping the shaft just above the spike with your other hand. Forget the crampons. For now, plain boots will do.

Slide on your belly, feet aimed downhill. Let your speed build, then gradually press the pick into the snow. In really soft snow you can ram the pick in all at once, but try the same in hard-pack or on ice and the grabbing tool will wrench from your hands. Dig your toes (again, no crampons) into the slope at the same time as you apply the pick brake. Arch your body so your belly is off the snow and your full weight comes onto the pick and your toes.

Repeat several times, varying your sliding speed until you get a feel for how the axe brakes.

Next, lie on your back, feet pointed downhill. Slide and get your momentum going, then flip or roll onto your belly and apply the pick and toes. Roll onto the side holding the pick (if the pick is in your right hand, your right shoulder hits the slope first).

You won't always have the luxury of braking with your dominant hand, so switch and practice self-arresting by pressing the pick in with your weak hand.

You may or may not have your crampons on when you fall, so you'll need to practice both ways. Put on your crampons and self-arrest. In relatively soft snow, like the kind you're practicing in, you can let the front points drag. On hard snow and ice, bend your knees and keep your front points in the air. If you let them dig in, you'll either cartwheel or wrench your ankles out of joint. This goes against instinct, so practice.

The party is over. Back on your belly, but this time slide headfirst. To self-arrest in this position, push the pick into the snow by your side and hold the shaft braced across your body about hip level. You needn't do anything else. The braking action of the pick will spin you around into the regular self-arrest position.

Last, lie on your back, head downhill. Brake as before, pick pressed into the snow near your hip, axe braced across your waist. Once again, the grabbing pick will spin you. Once your feet are downhill, flip into the regular self-arrest position.

Back self-arrest

The Changing Medium

Think of ice as a hoary beast, continually shape-shifting to the effects of sun, wind, snow, and temperature. A climb can be a stroll one day, but catch it in a mood swing after a week of warm weather and it can be a real gripper.

Snow is the same way. Catch consolidated, firm conditions, and, by blending French technique with front-pointing, you'll romp up that couloir or snowfield without breaking a sweat. Go when the time isn't right, and you'll either wallow in loose snow up to your waist, or struggle with sticky snow that balls up under your crampons.

Catching good snow and ice conditions is, to a small degree, a matter of luck, but more of it is recognizing the different conditions, when they are likely to be at their best, and attacking then. Still, you won't always have a choice — you may be on a mountain or route, and weather or time constraints may require that you climb what's in front of you, and right now. Do what you must.

Mike O'Donnell on chandeliered ice in Ouray, Colorado.

Ice types, conditions, and formations

Early and end-of-season ice is generally thin, warm, and wet. Difficult to lead and nearly impossible to protect, this ice is also unstable and prone to collapsing. Stay away until you've had years of schooling.

Cauliflower ice, the lumps and curls that form low-angle cones and staircases at the bottom of routes, is usually a gift. French technique with your feet, stepping onto the top of each lump. Holster one or both of your tools and "rock climb" by grabbing behind the horns. Alternately, set your picks over the curls and hook them. If the cauliflower is too sugary or malformed to hook, swing and plant your tools in the good ice over the crest.

Hooking also works well for hollow and rotten ice. Set your tools in natural pockets, slots, or holes. Lacking those, tap a hole and hook in this, or drag the pick down until it catches. Hook placements may seem dicey, but are usually solid as long as you don't climb too high on the tool and lever it out. Ideally, you'll be able to bury the pick to the head. When that isn't possible, remember, the shallower the hook, the steadier and lower you'll need to stay on the tool.

Bluish-white ice is the dream stuff. You usually find this "plastic" midseason, when routes are fat and temperatures stable. Plastic ice is one of the best media to learn on. It absorbs tools with single, light taps, fractures little, and protects well.

White, granulated ice is old and rotted by the sun. This ice is easy to climb — tools sink to the hilt with little effort — but a devil to protect because screws and hammer-ins lift out as easily as they push in.

In very cold temperatures, ice gets brittle and climbing it is like trying to swat a fly off a window with a hammer. Easy does it. Razor-sharp tools are a must. More than ever, focus on perfect technique and use swift, decisive strokes, or you'll pull the climb down around you. When a good pick placement seems impossible, bash away the first couple inches of surface ice. Often, the underlying ice, being insulated from the cold, is in better shape. If someone has climbed ahead of you, try hooking your tools in their placement holes, peg-board style.

Verglas is ice 1/4-inch to a couple of inches thick, and you climb it like brittle ice. Have sharp tools, stay on top of your form, and seek out lumps that will hold the most steel. Get your plants on the first swing, or carve nicks with light, tapping strikes, and work the features like you would on rock. Thin ice itself is typically unprotectable, but, hopefully, the rock around it will take gear.

Warm days and cold nights are a recipe for chandelier ice, the stuff Munch was thinking of when he painted "The Scream." You often run into this unstable medium early in the season on newly formed flows. Chandelier ice consists of pencil-sized icicles that rake away under the lightest touch, revealing more of the same underneath. Worse, it tends to form in curtains, with each tier overhanging the one below it. Protection and solid plants are rare, as are climbers who like to lead this garbage. You can sometimes climb chandelier ice by lightly setting the tools in the creases between the larger icicles. Usually, though, you have to plant the tools high and drag them down until they catch. Then pull and watch your teeth.

Free climbing cauliflower ice

Snow types and conditions

Neve is old, hard snow that feels like ice, or has actually consolidated into it. Look for neve in the backs of chimneys and gullies, and on low-angle slopes near the end of winter, when the sun and wind have had time to consolidate the

Scour away surface snow and rotten ice to get at the solid, underlying ice.

snow pack. Because neve takes so long to form, it isn't likely to change much from day to day. Generic neve is soft and relatively easy to climb and protect. It's best to tackle neve early in the morning, before the sun softens it.

Styrofoam ice, the squeaky, tool- and protection-eating stuff, behaves and feels more like hard snow than soft ice, and it can actually be better than either medium. As with neve, mountain conditions are suited to brewing a good batch of styrofoam, which tends to form on low-angle slopes, although vertical pitches of it aren't unusual. Also like neve, styrofoam is slow to change consistency.

Snow that sticks to your crampons is wet because the sun has melted it, it fell wet and hasn't had time to dry out, or it has rained. Sticky snow sucks at your feet and builds up on your boots like wet concrete, clogging the tread or crampons, and making the going slippery and dangerous. Spend much — or a little — time struggling in it and you'll learn that it is best to avoid it by going earlier in the morning or later in the evening or night, when the snow is colder and drier.

Loose snow is what you'd think: loose, unconsolidated snow. Not bad, provided it is only a couple inches deep, but beyond boot depth it gets laborious to move in, not to mention the increase in avalanche danger. You'll find loose snow, naturally, just after a snowfall and on the leeward side of ridges. If you are "lucky" and the snow is only knee-deep or so, you can posthole. Deeper than that and you'll have to clear or shovel a trough ahead of you. Switch leads often to keep the worker up front fresh.

Breakable crust would be better named heart-breakable crust. This crust forms over loose snow. It holds your weight for an instant, getting you to think you are in for an easy step, then gives way. Breakable crust is frustrating and strenuous to deal with. Dodge it by travelling early or late, when the firmed-up crust is likely to hold body weight.

Taking the Lead

The ice was thunker plastic the day Jim and I trudged up to The Fang, a 100-foot, free-hanging pillar above Vail, Colorado. Jim had never led such steep, unrelenting ice, but he had been following for a week straight and hadn't faltered. That, and the good ice conditions, had me thinking that maybe it was time for him to up the ante.

"What do you think?" I asked.

"I'll give it a shot," he said with a little tremolo as he took the rope.

He smoked the first 30 feet, but once he got some real air under him, his tools began slapping the ice cockeyed and his crampons sheared out. When he got high enough that his last piece of pro was useless, he began vibrating like the front end of an old VW bus.

"Hang in there," I called up, "You're doing good."

A wail was his only response. I paced at the belay, mentally flogging myself for getting him in this predicament.

"Get a screw in," I screamed, now fearing the worst — a 50-foot air-fall onto a jagged ice cone.

Quebec climber Stephanne Lapierre on one of Pont Rouge's megaclassic one-pitchers.

"I can't," he sobbed.

Jim's brain seized into a bloodless cube. He hung limp from his tools. Both feet dangled free of the ice. One of his tools popped. "Ahh..." he moaned.

I don't know if it was my yelling, but he sprang to life. Resetting his crampons and tool, he twisted in a screw, clipped the rope, and lowered. He hasn't led ice since.

Tying into the sharp end of the rope isn't for everyone. Too much pressure. Too much danger. Some climbers never get experienced or comfortable enough to lead ice. Those climbers shouldn't even try — Jim barely held it together, and until then he was stone solid.

Don't get cocky. Most ice and snow climbs are strolls — on toprope — but as soon as you tie in to the sharp end you're playing a different game. Get pumped and you can't "take." Get scared and there is no overhead rope to console you.

Leading ice and snow is only for expert, confident climbers who have already mastered leading on rock. They already know how to fiddle in natural gear, and know the penalty for getting strung out. If you can't lead rock and place pins, nuts, and cams, don't even contemplate leading a steep snowslope or ice. These nefarious media are far more finicky than rock; the pro is more difficult to get and often dubious, and the consequences of a fall are severe. The best protection on snow and ice is not to fall, period.

Despite leading's hazards, most everyone will be driven to it sooner or later. The call to test your mettle is natural. Ease into it. Learn to lead on toprope.

Getting a rack

You're just starting out, but you don't want to be a slacker by relying on your partner for all the gear. A dozen pieces or so is plenty for a starter rack, and will protect a long pitch and the belay. Also, don't neglect to throw in a token rock rack. Often, in narrow gullies or slender pillars, you can find good protection in the rock next to or behind the ice, or you may need rock gear to set up a belay. A set of nuts and cams and a handful of assorted pitons is usually plenty. Tubular screws, hammer-ins, and hooks are the three types of ice protection. You'll need a mix, but

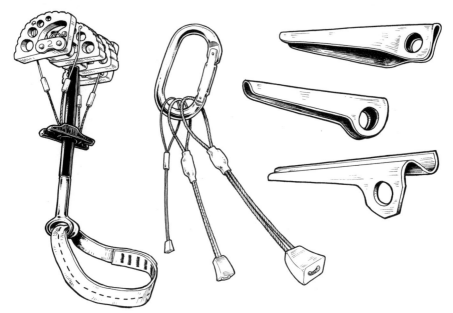

Cams, nuts, and pitons complement and often are the backbone of the ice rack

go heavy on screws. These are the most versatile, working in warm and brittle conditions where hammer-ins can wiggle out or shatter the ice.

When shopping for screws — and all ice pro — buy name brands. Stay away from mystery protection. Such pieces may save you a couple of bucks, but who knows if they'll hold? Select three or so screws of various lengths, and augment this with a couple of hammer-ins. Hammer-ins are faster to place than screws, making them great for leading, but are tricky to remove.

Ice hooks are what you'd imagine: big steel talons with terrible barbs. Hooks won't usually hold as well as screws or hammer-ins, but are great for mixed climbing because you can set them in ice too thin for other gear, or pound them into the rock like a piton.

Carabiners and slings

Ice climbing requires carabiners of all types, but mostly you'll want regular Ds for clipping pro, rigging belays, and so on, and enough ovals — a minimum of four — for carabiner-brake rappels when the rope is too frozen to feed through a rappel device. Have at least one large, screw-gate locking carabiner to use with your belay device and for rappelling.

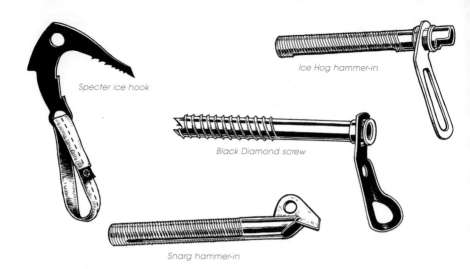

Specter ice hook

Ice Hog hammer-in

Black Diamond screw

Snarg hammer-in

Locking 'biner

Do not use the spring-loaded or self-locking carabiners, as their locking mechanisms jam with ice and snow.

You'll need quickdraws and slings every time you place protection, set up a belay, and rappel. Carry enough sewn quickdraws so you have one for each piece of protection. Beyond that, don't leave the house without at least a half-dozen over-the-shoulder runners. Make these tied, not sewn. Tied runners are slightly bulkier, but you can untie them to thread around trees, chockstones, and icicles.

Snow pro

If you intend to venture beyond roadside ice crags and into the mountains, you'll need pickets or deadmen, the two types of snow anchors. Pickets are two- to three-foot-long aluminum stakes, made from either T or angle stock, that you hammer into dense, consolidated snow. These are fairly basic. Look for a pointed end to facilitate driving the picket into

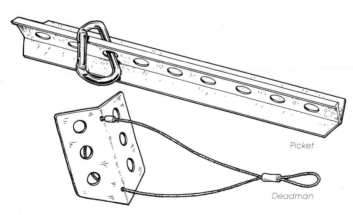

Picket

Deadman

hard snow, and lightening holes for clipping the anchor flush to the snow surface.

A deadman, or "fluke," is a large, shovel-sized plate of aluminum, bent in the middle, and swaged with a long cable loop. Deadmen work in loose snow, where pickets would shear out. Their large surface area and kite-like design give them their holding power; when you load one, it planes deeper into the snow. The harder you pull, the deeper it goes. Deadmen come in two sizes: small for hardpack and large for powder conditions. The better deadmen have reinforced striking surfaces and load-lightening holes.

Leading ice

Unless you want to solo every route, you must master placing ice screws and hammer-ins. You've learned a bit of this by cleaning your experienced partner's gear, but go to your local ice bouldering area and polish the routine. Place the gear while both feet are planted safely on the ground, then boulder up a couple of feet and stick in a piece.

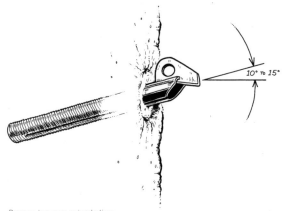

To place a screw or hammer-in, first take your tool and use the pick or adze to scour away any rotten or fractured surface ice. Ice protection is only as solid as the ice *Proper ice-pro orientation* itself, so clear until you find the solid, uniform base ice.

Now take your tool and gouge a pilot hole about an inch deep and angled slightly down. Stab the piece into the hole and finish hammering or screwing it, trying to keep the outside end angled slightly uphill 10 to 15 degrees so any loading will cam the piece into the ice. Note any sudden change in resistance as the screw or hammer-in goes in. A placement that gets noticeably easier to twist or drive has hit an air pocket or section of bad ice. Consider it suspect.

Set gear with your right hand, then try it with the left.

QUICK-DRAW SCREWS

Monkeying with the rope, slings, and carabiners is tricky when you're wearing gloves or mittens. Reduce fumbling by racking each screw and hammer-in on its own quickdraw, and use bent-gate carabiners on the rope-clip end. Organize the rack before you head up. Move the gear you think you'll need first to the front of your gear sling. Rack ice pro on large bent-gates that let you whip off a piece simply by pressing its hanger against the gate.

Before you start leading, you'll want to be ambidextrous with the gear — the ice won't always let you set protection with your dominant hand, and even when it does, switching hands spreads the pump.

Examine the ice and remember its condition relative to how good the piece was. Ice will never be the same twice. It pays to visit the bouldering crag frequently and place pro in all conditions, from wet soft ice to brittle, fracturing garbage.

Once you are confident you can get good gear in all situations and conditions, find a route you think you could lead, then hike around and set a toprope on it. Now "lead" and practice placing gear. Trail a second rope and simulate the clips as well. Block out the safety of the overhead rope and imagine you are really on the sharp end. Ask yourself, "where can I rest, where can I get gear, do I trust that tool placement, is the protection good?"

Finish the route, then lower off and, to give you a feel for the reliability of the screws you placed, clean them on your way down. "Lead" the route on toprope several times, then lower your sights and find an easier route for you to actually lead. No shame.

Find your prospective lead — nothing serious, pick a slabby flow for now — then rappel it and pre-place the gear. Set a good screw or hammer-in every eight or 10 feet.

Tie in and dance up the route, clipping the gear as you go, same as you would on a bolted sport climb. Go smooth and steady. The worst thing you can do is to get impatient or panic.

You did great. You kept your head, balanced over your feet, and cruised the route. Do it one more time and you're ready to clean that gear and place it again, this time when it counts.

Tips for setting protection

Burly arms are certainly an asset for placing protection, but the real trick is choosing your stances carefully. Lead with your head, not your arms.

Climb to nearby ramps or shelves and set the gear off those good stances. Likewise, stem in corners and chimneys to unweight your tools. On low-angle alpine ice, where you use tools for balance more than pulling on, setting protection isn't much of an issue, though you should still look for breaks in the angle, and set your gear there.

Dangling on a sheet of steep ice and whacking in gear is the least desirable. It is also unavoidable, so get used to it. Here, it helps to be efficient and confident, and to have a system. Many ice climbers attach daisy chains to their harnesses, then clip these to the tools and hang, freeing both hands to set gear

Learn to set protection single handedly

at leisure. Purists eschew this practice, calling it aid, but the real reason you needn't get in the habit is because it is slow. Few climbers can use this technique efficiently. All that frigging with ropes, daisy chains, and carabiners takes all day.

Another technique involves loosening one wrist loop and sliding your arm through it so you can hang off the elbow, freeing the hand to help with the pro. This method works well, provided you can loosen and tighten your wrist loop at leisure. Its only drawbacks are it takes two extra steps (loosening and retightening the wrist loop) and, unless you make a conscious effort not to, it causes you to pull out on the axe, increasing its likelihood of popping.

A better option is the simple one: Learn to hang from one wrist loop and set gear with the other hand — on long routes it's the only way you'll get to the top before you freeze or the thing falls down.

Even when done quickly, one-arm placements are strenuous. Ease the burden by chopping a small step about waist level. Climb onto it, and then stand with one foot flat, a more relaxing position than all-out front points, and set the gear from that position. Step or no, get comfortable, feet spread and weight over them. Before you start the placement, make dead certain the tool you will hang from is solid. Plant it well. Take your hammer and bash the axe to the hilt if necessary.

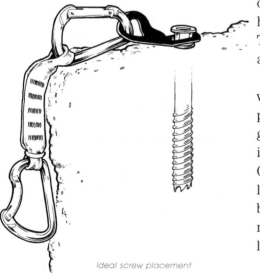

Ideal screw placement

Blink, breathe, contemplate where you'll set the gear. Don't place gear too high. Overhead gives you a secure, toprope feeling for a few moves, but is tiring. Chest level is about right. Waist level is better still because it lets blood flow freely to the arm, is the most relaxing, and gives you more leverage for placing a screw.

Do not place gear on the crest of

bulges. The whole corner section could shear off. Also avoid setting hammer-ins between icicles or in grooves. Though tempting targets, these are the most difficult of all places to remove gear, requiring major chopping to clear a turning radius for the hanger. The ideal placements are near the back of steps, or over and behind bulges, positions that increase the gear's pull-out strength.

Gripped? You should be. Any slip and you'll break both ankles and wrists, or your neck, or impale yourself on a jagged blade. Being gripped is OK. Being scared numb isn't. If you feel the onset of panic, drop an ice hook in the high slot left by your hammer. Tap the hook with your hand to set it, then give it a couple smacks with the hammer and clip in the rope. Now you can settle down and place the real pro.

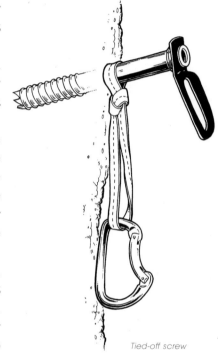

Tied-off screw

Drive or screw the piece to the eye, but be careful not to bottom out against rock or you'll bugger the end of the pro, especially if it is made of aluminum or titanium. When a placement won't go to the eye, tie it off.

How often you stop and put in gear is your call. A couple of pieces a pitch on low-angle ice can suffice, while on vertical ice a placement every couple of body lengths is ideal, but not always practical. The ice could be rotten, your arms may be too flamed to hang out, you're in a dangerous ice-fall path and need to move quickly, and so on. Putting in gear is strenuous, usually more so than climbing, and you may want to run it out. Inexperienced or frightened leaders, though, tend to seize up and move at a snail's pace when they get far above gear. Those climbers will find that spacing gear closely is faster — and safer — in the long haul. Much of the time you won't have a choice; the ice quality or topography will

Michael Kennedy prepares to set a screw on a free-hanging icicle in Box Canyon, Colorado.

dictate where the protection goes. Bad ice, for example, may force you to run it out higher to better ice. Stepped ice, where any fall will likely be onto a ledge, demands closely set gear.

All too often a climber will carefully protect the route, then run it out like a madman the last 20 or 30 feet. This is a huge mistake. Run it out to just below the top if you must, then put in gear. If you're going to fall, it will probably be while you are pulling over the top, where the ice is thinnest and you are the most pumped. For those reasons, even when the exit looks trivial, set a screw in the good ice right below it. You never know, the entire top sheet could slide off with you on it.

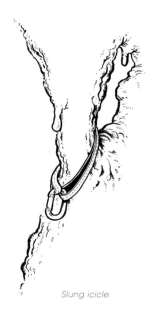

Slung icicle

Finally, don't think of screws and hammer-ins as your only forms of protection. Sling icicles and drop runners over cauliflowers or lumps that you've incut with your axe. These natural anchors can be strong, take little time and effort to rig, and save your rack. Also take advantage of the rock behind or next to the ice.

On some pillar routes, you can climb part way up the rock wall behind the ice, set good rock gear there, then down-climb and cruise up the ice, slyly protected by the rock gear. In gullies, climb close to one of the side walls and you might find all of your protection in the rock.

Leading snow

Being on the sharp end of the rope on snow isn't nearly as involved or tedious as it is on ice, but don't take this as an excuse to dive in, inexperienced and headfirst. Get proficient at self-arresting, start out on easy slopes, and get in mileage before tackling Denali.

Before you start leading up a snow face or gully, you should first ask yourself if roping up is prudent. Climbing unroped, using your axe and self-arrest skills as belays, lets you move quickly, always an advantage in the mountains. Soloing big, exposed faces, however, can be intimidating to the point

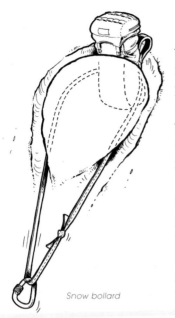

Snow bollard

where it can be faster to break out the rope and tack confidently along setting pickets and flukes than to tentatively poke about, fearing for your life. Same goes when there's a dangerous drop or crevasse directly below, and when dehydration, fatigue, or altitude have you addled.

Roping up braces your courage, but unless you are willing to stop and put in protection, or snow conditions are too poor to hold protection, the rope is false security. If either member falls, both are likely to get dragged down the face. Break out the rope and you better get good anchors, those being the bollard, deadman (also called a fluke), and picket.

The bollard is the snow equivalent of a slung rock horn. It is an all-natural anchor that you construct by carving a circular, incut trench in the snow and looping the rope around the stump you've created. Snow firmness and bollard diameter determine its strength. You may, in soft snow, have to build bollards five feet in diameter (or larger), while in hard snow you may only have to go a foot or two across. Experience will give you a feel for what works in what conditions. Regardless, cut any bollard at least a foot deep, and incut the walls so the rope can't slide out.

A bollard will fail because the rope shears through it like a cheese cutter. When this is a possibility, pad the back of the bollard with your jacket or pack, or wrap the rope around the bollard as many times as necessary to distribute the stress. If you are using the bollard as a rappel anchor, scrounge rocks or chunks of firmer snow or ice, and line the bollard with these.

Deadmen are shovel-blade-like aluminum plates that you drive into the snow. A deadman's broad surface area gives it its holding power, as does its angled face, which serves as a dynamic diving plane. The benefits are twofold: The diving action gradually absorbs the force, and, lodges the plate even deeper.

Buried layers of crust or ice can cause a deadman to skip out, and in powder snow a deadman can drag for a moment then shear through. Despite these disadvantages, deadmen are, in soft snow, often the only anchor that has a chance of holding.

Placing deadmen is tricky. You don't just plop one in the snow and expect it to hold.

Deadman

The correct placement calls for cutting a T-slot in the snow and pounding the deadman into this at a 45-degree angle. Make sure the deadman's swaged cable sticks out through the bottom leg of the T, and that the angle of pull drives the deadman deeper — set the angle too steep or shallow and the piece will pop out rather than dive. Give the deadman a good test tug to make sure you've got everything right.

Pickets are essentially giant tent stakes you pound into the snow. Pickets don't have the dynamic load-absorbing ability of deadmen, but they are quicker and simpler to set, and their resistance to being driven into the snow gives you a good indication of how solid or shaky they are. Use a picket as you'd think. Angle it away from the anticipated direction of pull, whack it into the snow and, to reduce leverage, clip the hole nearest the snow surface.

As on ice, how often you stop and put in protection depends on many factors, including slope steepness and snow conditions. More likely it will depend on how much protection you are carrying. If you only have a couple of pickets and a deadman, you'll set two pieces on the lead and reserve one to back up your ice axe at the belay. In any case, remember, if you neglect to put in protection the rope is of little value.

Bringing up the Rear

The fastest route to becoming a competent leader is to become a competent follower. Do that by paying attention. When the leader is climbing, watch. Don't cower in a wet hole listening to the ice crash and bemoaning the horror that awaits. Evaluate your leader's every move. Why did he place that screw where he did? Why did he choose that path?

Why is he hooking? Watch his footwork and body position, and compare it to how you might have climbed that section. Visualize.

Let it flow, Joe

Climb in control. Rush or get swept with fear, and you'll flame out. You won't be able to think. You'll flounder, have a miserable time. Get into the groove. Don't be afraid to call for a snug rope if you need it, but never "take" just because you are tired. Be decisive with your tools and, as always, stay on your feet.

Let the flow of the ice determine your rhythm. Rest on lower-angle sections or in stems, and bore ahead when the

On longer routes, "draft" by setting your tools in the leader's tool slots.

ice is steep and unrelenting. On longer routes or delicate lines where there's barely enough ice to hold the tools, or when you're in a dangerous rock, ice, or avalanche zone and speed is paramount, try drafting. Bicycle and auto racers edge up behind the leader's rear tire and use the pocket of dead air there to coast along relatively free of wind-resistance. To draft on ice, simply set your picks in the slots already carved by the leader. No need to swing. Hooking like this won't give you a feel for the ice, but it is almost effortless (provided you relax) and fast.

When you can't find or follow the leader's cut marks, or you otherwise want the experience of making your own placements, go ahead and slam in the tools. Set them deep, then, as you get a feel for the ice, set them lighter, then lighter still. Find that fine line where the tools are easy to place, yet still solid.

Don't be afraid to experiment, but, again, watch your dental work and make sure the leader knows when you are going off a dubious test placement.

Getting the gear out

Remove screws and other protection from convenient stances. Usually these will be the same stances the leader

Toot

STAYING SHARP

Crampons and ice tools have one thing in common: They are inefficient and dangerous when dull. Dull points take more effort to push into the ice than sharp ones, and, worse, they shatter the ice, slip, and skate out.

Sharpen your tools when you see that they are getting dull, well before they have gone blunt. Touching up an edge is far easier than manufacturing a new one.

Use two files for sharpening. A six-inch mill bastard file works well on crampon points and tool blades. The other file is a 3/16-inch round chainsaw file, which you use to sharpen the front pick teeth. Forget a bench grinder. It takes off too much metal and can get a pick red-hot, ruining the temper.

Pick modification

Sharpening tools is basic. You use the same techniques here as for your trusty jackknife. Remove only enough metal to get the tool sharp. The tips of your axe and hammer blades are double-beveled. File each side equally, using the manufacturer's bevel as a guide. Go slow and check your angle every couple licks. Make the edge sharp, but don't get it paper-thin or it will bend over.

The top side of your picks may also need sharpening, but this depends on the pick design. Most piolets have squared, blunt top edges that never need sharpening, but nearly all technical tools can benefit from honing the leading four or five inches of the top edge. Doing so gives the pick a thinner profile, letting it slice into the ice with minimal fracturing and effort, and facilitating tool removal.

"Sticky" picks, those that are hard to remove no matter how lightly you set them in the ice, will benefit from beveling the teeth. Go easy here. Strop the teeth just a little, then take them bouldering for a test run. File sticky teeth further still, then try them out again.

Sharpen crampon side- and front points as needed, being careful to retain the manufacturer's bevel, which was carefully selected for the point configuration.

used to set the gear, but occasionally you may be able to climb a move higher or scoot a little to the side and find a more advantageous or restful position. On steep ice where there is no stance, I like to climb until the piece is about chest level, then remove it.

Ice screws are easy to get out. Simply unscrew them. Unseat a hook with a carefully placed upward tap, then lift it out. Hammer-ins are the real buggers. These you'll have to partly chop out, then unscrew. A common mistake is to start unscrewing too early, with the hammer-in still binding in the hole. Blast away a good two inches of ice before trying to turn the piece, and if it still resists, chop away even more.

A screw or hammer-in may freeze into place and refuse to

budge. When this happens, give the head a couple sharp blows with the hammer. Driving the piece farther into the ice will jostle its bond, just as a rusted axle nut will loosen when you give it a good whack with a mallet.

Once the piece is free, try to clear out the ice plug inside it so it is ready to use again. Leave it in and it will set up like concrete, taking twice the effort to remove. Wet ice usually shakes or taps right out. Much of the time you can use the screw or hammer-in as a blowtube and purge the plug with a guttural puff. (Don't put your lips to the metal if it's really cold out — remember the tongue-stuck-to-the-flagpole incident back in second grade?) If a quick shake, tap, or blow doesn't work, clip the piece to your gear sling and deal with the plug at the belay, where you can use two hands.

Is it safe?

Killer Pillars

You've been dreaming about this day ever since you spent your retirement on ice gear and labored over a tedious how-to book. After a couple seasons of practice, those slabby flows that once seemed unsurmountable now have all the appeal of wet toast. Now it is time for a higher, loftier test. A free-hanging shaft of rocking blue ice, 100 feet vertical, capped by a squid of brittle tentacles, should suffice.

Let it begin.

Is it safe?

Several years ago, I was climbing a free-hanging pencil in Rifle, Colorado, when the identical climb next to it snapped off and came thundering down. The huge pillar didn't groan or creak, as I'd always imagined ice would do prior to cutting loose. It dropped suddenly, without warning. My knees nearly rattled me off the route I was on before I could beat it to the top and call it a day.

Today I think long and hard before tackling any ice that's in the sun — as those pillars were — or has been in the sun prior to my getting on it. I'll only climb on a cold day and when I'm certain the ice is solid.

No one can predict when a climb is or isn't safe, but you can be certain that sunny, warm days put you at more risk than crisp, cold ones. The sun and warming air undermine

PROTECTING YOUR PROTECTION

Ice pro is tenuous at best. Increase its chances of holding by using load-absorbing runners, such as "Screamers." Fall on one and the specially sewn break-away stitches activate to absorb 500 or so pounds of impact. With all the stitching blown out, the sling is still runner strength.

the all-important ice-to-rock bond. Without this glue, the integrity of the ice alone must support its substantial weight. Pillars that lie against the rock may be fine in these conditions, but don't count on it. I've seen those buckle like accordions and come tumbling down. Vertical ice that's pulled away from the rock, and free-hanging icicles, are the most dangerous.

Smaller pillars are, logically, more likely to shear off than fatter ones. Even in perfect conditions, those frail pillars, some no bigger around than a telephone pole, can break away simply from your added bodyweight or the fracturing effect of your tools. Assuming the climb doesn't collapse, there's another danger — you probably won't be getting in much, if any, gear. Don't fall.

Worse still are those stalks that don't touch the ground. While these represent cutting-edge ice climbing, they also present great danger. They fall down on a regular basis, and the protection, if you can get any, is even spottier than on the slender pillars.

Some climbers test the worthiness of ice pillars by thumping them hard with an ice axe. The resonance, and whether or not the climb falls down, tells them how sturdy the climb is. Better than nothing, I suppose.

Examine the ice. Horizontal fractures show that the pillar has tried to fall once already. That climb can still be safe as long as the crease has had time to melt, refreeze, and heal itself, but you never know. Chandeliered ice is perhaps the hairiest. Besides being unprotectable, you can often put your fist through the entire chandelier formation. Slushy, snow-cone ice, while easy to climb, is about as reliable as wet dry-wall. Smooth, blue ice is what you want, and the stickier the better. This stuff takes tools and gear with minimal pillar-weakening fractures.

Look, listen, and sniff the ice. You have good sense, use it. Never climb anything you are afraid to stand under.

Special equipment

You use the same gear on a pillar as you do on slabby flows: easy-to-swing, 40- to 50-centimeter, technical water-ice tools. Also carry a short third tool, holstered and at the ready.

For crampons, rigid is standard and mono points have several advantages. They shatter brittle ice less, and in thin or particularly delicate ice, you don't have to kick in the points — simply step in the slots already cut by your tools.

If you opt for these specialized front points, get the thin ones. Thick monos

Mono point

smash the ice worse than two regular vertical points. Tube-type monos are worst of all.

Wear gaiters, not so much to keep the snow out of your boots, but so you can watch your feet and, when your feet have to be close together, as they often are on a slender pillar, so you won't snag your breeches. And, as always, wear sticky-palm gloves or thin mitts that let you easily operate carabiners.

Pillar climbing is like busting rocks with a sledge, a torrid activity. Don't overdress. Wear all that pile and shell gear and you're in for a real melt-fest. Dress light but appropriate to conditions. On a drippy climb with air temperatures just under freezing, long underwear and shell gear are plenty.

Moving

Pillar routes demand a keener sense of tool handling than those plump ramps you're used to. Put the crosshairs on each placement and go easy. Set the tools just enough to hold. An inch of pick is plenty solid in good ice. Be precise and calculating with your tools and crampons. Clear away the rotten or loose surface ice, but try to maintain a "quiet" presence. Watch a good pillar climber and you'll be surprised how little ice he knocks down, even when conditions are bad.

On large, industrial smoke-stack-sized pillars, place your tools and feet wherever they are comfortable and keep you in balance. Narrow popsicles require a different tack. Here, set the placements where they will do the least damage.

Minimum impact icicle climbing

Often, you'll want to place the advancing tool high and directly above the one you're pulling on. Place the tools side-by-side or too close together and the pillar could fracture from pick to pick.

Brittle or otherwise delicate formations call for the surgeon's touch. Best not to hit the ice at all. Hook your tools in melt holes or over cauliflowers. Shimmy up the ice by grabbing nodules and goiters with your hands, and by wrapping your legs, or whatever is required, around the shaft, or by heel hooking.

Step and press, rather than kick, your crampons. Mono points are a boon here — concentrating all the weight on one point sets it deep. If you must kick or swing, take light pecks and aim for obvious weaknesses, like vertical creases, and trust in minimal contact.

Pillars that don't reach the ground represent the greatest challenge. Sometimes you can climb an ice smear on the wall behind the tooth, and then lean over or stem onto the pillar. Most of the time, however, the wall behind the hanging tooth is bare, crumbling rock. Climb this garbage as best you can until you are high enough to swing out and onto the ice. When the entrance onto the ice is barred by icicles, rake them away now with your axe, rather than, in a moment, with your head. Use the same tactic anytime you have to climb out from under a toothed roof or overlap.

You'll find that the hardest ice moves are the first few. You may even be dead-hanging from one tool and no feet. Burly climbers can one-arm and muscle in the next placement. The weaker of us will want to stack the tools by hooking the free one over the top of the planted one. Though funky feeling, this position lets you use both arms to pull up.

Don't overlook the kneebar or heel-toe. You can often wedge a knee or boot between the lip of the ice and the rock, or even between two icicles, making it relatively effortless to advance your tools.

You've climbed up rock as high as you can and you still can't reach the ice. You'll either have to bag it or try leaning and levering off a tool shaft, the pick of which is either set behind or undercingling an incut in the rock. Don't be afraid to try this, provided the protection is good. Lever off the shaft, keep your body tight and straight, and you'll be able to swipe out with the free tool six, maybe eight feet.

Stacked tools

Now what? You're spread-eagled and staring at one doozy of a swing when you cut free from the rock. What to do? Make sure your belayer is attentive and the photographer has plenty of film, then go for it. Don't flop like overcooked pasta. Keep your body tense to check the swing and use the momentum to bury your other tool in the ice. Wallow and advance the tools any way you can.

Often, the rock behind the ice is the key to the route.

Belaying

"Ahh, shizze, yaaaa, watch it you ...." Comments from the belay had taken a nasty tone. Mark Herndon was teed. We were halfway up the Triolet North Face, and he was really taking a beating, but not from climbing. I was leading above him, and every time I slammed a tool in the brittle ice, a big chunk of it would plate off and scream down the face, right into Mark.

"Shut up," I yelled, unsympathetic. "Can't you see I'm leading?"

I jacked in the axe. Another bollock of ice punched Mark like a steel fist.

"You're killing me," he screamed.

I was indeed, and that day we both learned one of the fundamentals of ice climbing: Never belay directly under the leader.

Where to belay

Ice is heavy. A lump as small as a golf ball can brain you or break bones. Always protect the belayer. Establish the belay well clear of the ice- and rock-fall zone.

Seek out large potholes, caves, overhangs, or the underside of a bulge — anyplace that offers shelter from falling debris. Lacking a suitable deflector, traverse off route and

Eric DeCamp and Catherine Destivelle on the 3000-foot Namche Bazaar icefall, Nepal.

Stay heads up when you belay ice.

place the belay far to one side, or, as a last resort, have the belayer get small under the padding of a rucksack. Even in the best places the belayer isn't completely safe. I've watched ice bounce and pop my belayer, even though she was standing a good 40 feet to the side.

Burrowing in a sheltered belay does bring up a problem: Tucked safely away, you can't see or hear the leader. Let the rope be your antenna. When it feeds steadily out, the leader is probably climbing. When it stops, she is setting a piece or negotiating a nasty section. Brace yourself when the rope starts quivering.

Try to stay warm and psyched at the belay. This isn't easy. Have a sip of hot tea. Pull out the down jacket and crawl into it. I sometimes sing Ring of Fire, or tell myself it's really tomorrow and I'm on the sofa stroking my paunch.

Belay devices

Forget any device that can jam with snow or ice, doesn't work on a frozen rope, or doesn't double as a rappel device. Get either a Sticht- or Tuber-style plate or a Figure-8 with a small hole designed for belaying.

Figure-8

Sticht plate

Tuber

Greg Child at a belay on the North Face of Mount Hunter.

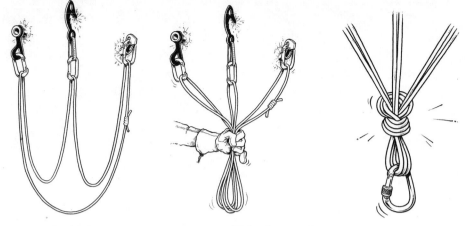

Cordelette

Belaying on ice

The ideal, obvious belay is a large ledge, 150 feet up, with two, old-growth sequoias sprouting from it. Don't count on finding that, but do count on always rigging a bomber station, no matter what the ice conditions.

Consider two solid anchors the minimum. Any fewer and you're rolling the bones. Large trees or nuts and pins in good rock are your best bets. Lacking those, you'll have to set anchors in the ice.

"But the ice is all rotten," you say, "no go with the belay anchors." Hogwash. If the ice was solid enough for you to climb, it is solid enough — at least somewhere — for you to set good anchors. Take an axe and chop away the bad ice until you hit paydirt. Keep climbing or traverse — another reason to use an extra long rope — when the ice near that comfortable ledge is no good. Find the good ice and belay there.

Arrange the anchors the same as you would on rock: logically and equalized. Place one screw, clip the rope to it, and then, if the ice topography permits, place a second screw a couple of feet from the first. In brittle ice, spread out the screws farther still to prevent the ice from fracturing across from screw to screw. When the ice is too funky to set two screws next to each other, climb or traverse to a place where the ice will take a second screw. Set that screw, clip the rope to it, and reverse back to the first belay screw. Use the rope and slings to string the anchors together in an equalized or quasi-equalized manner. To make rigging belays a snap, savvy ice climbers carry a "cordelette," a 20-foot length of 7mm perlon, and use this to rig the belay.

As a last precaution, bury both tools nearby and clip yourself to them with runners.

Belaying on snow

The sitting hip-belay, boot-axe belay, and direct-axe belay are the three fundamental methods for belaying in snow. Snow conditions and slope angle will tell you which to use.

Hip belay

Work the sitting hip-belay the same as you would for rock. Brace yourself and rely on a solid position and the friction of the rope wound around your body to catch falls. Fight the temptation to use a belay device. These are slower to set up and give a more static catch than the hip-belay, making it more likely that you'll get jerked from the stance. Catching a fall on snow depends on your letting the rope slip, then gradually applying the brakes.

In its simplest form, the hip-belay consists of wedging yourself in a shallow moat or crevasse, bracing against the backside of a boulder or ridge, or digging a deep seat in the snow and plopping down in it. Use a back-up anchor any time your stance is less than totally bomber.

Boot-axe belay

In soft, unconsolidated snow, plop down on your duff and wiggle or dig a nice, deep seat. Trench in, facing out and legs pointed downhill. Use your body like a well-rooted fence post, braced to catch the fall. The feet-downhill position may seem backward for belaying a leader, but is correct. If the leader rips out all the protection (a possibility), the force will come onto you from below. If the protection stays put, the upward pull on you won't amount to much anyway; the low angle will see to that.

Strengthen your position by ramming the axe shaft into the snow next to your hip. Bury the axe to the head, keeping the pick pointed away from you. Now make a hip-axe belay by passing the rope around your body and the axe shaft.

The hip-axe belay works fine in soft snow, but firm snow necessitates the boot-axe belay. Set up by first driving the axe shaft, pick pointed across the slope, into the snow all the way to the head. When the snow is too hard to bury the tool by hand, stomp or pound on the axe head to drive it in.

Orient yourself so you face across the slope. Plant your uphill foot next to the axe shaft so the two touch and can support one another. Keep your weight centered over this uphill foot. Your downhill foot

Carabiner-axe belay

is for balance only. Now, flip the rope over your uphill boot and around the axe shaft. Hold the axe in place by pushing down on the head with your uphill hand. Your downhill hand works the rope by shuffling it along.

If your partner falls onto the boot-axe belay, push down hard on the axe, wait for the impact to come onto it and your boot, let the rope slip to absorb energy, then wind the rope across your ankle and gradually tighten down. Don't panic and try to catch the fall all at once. As with the hip-axe belay, giving an intentional dynamic belay is key to not getting plucked off the face.

A similar, but more restful boot-axe belay is the standing carabiner-axe belay, which you effect by passing the axe shaft through a large locking carabiner, stomping the axe into the snow, and standing with both feet holding the axe in place. Pass the lead rope through the carabiner, and hip belay as usual. As you'll quickly learn, the carabiner-axe belay is easier on your back than the stooped over method, and just as effective.

When snow gets so hard that you can no longer bury the axe shaft for a boot-axe station, shift to the direct axe belay. To do this, bury the axe pick — pound it in with the second tool if necessary — and clip yourself into the wrist loop, which must be runner strength. As a backup, slam in the second tool and clip to it. Brace yourself and use the hip-belay to keep things dynamic.

Rob Milne in typical mixed conditions in the Cairngorms, Scotland.

Mixed Emotions

Avocado Gully is one of western Colorado's Grade III ice romps. When it's ice, that is. This time it needed another week or two of filling out. But you do it anyway. Tools planted in mush. Who knows what keeps them in? You drag them down until they catch, then move on. Front points quiver on sloping rock. Have to keep the legs steady, son, it's no time to get spastic. Fist jammed in a watery crack. Then a chockstone hook. Then a butt plant. Then a knee wedge. Shake off one mitt and barehand a cold incut. Crampon skates — grreeee — heart hurts as the load comes onto the chockstone. It holds, blessed be. Pull over the top with eyes on fire and wild hair. Beautiful.

There's nothing like a bout of mixed climbing to pull everything together, focus your technique, and align your soul. By mixed, I mean that weird ground where you aren't certain if you are climbing rock, ice, or snow. You're usually sampling a tad of each: crampon on rock, one tool in ice, one hand counter-pressing on rock, the other boot and butt in snow. You grovel like a spider in a tub. Peck, peck, peck, slip, slip.

You gain progress in small, persistent increments. The protection is often spotty. The moves are obscure, and you usually only have a vague notion about what you'll do next. You just know that you'll do it. It's all in your head, and that's the hardest part.

Mixed climbing isn't for beginners. Attempt it only after you're well versed in ice and snow technique, and even then start easy — better still on toprope.

Dry tooling

For mixed climbing you use the same axe and hammer as on ice, but they work differently. Think of your tools as hooks, cams, and levers, rather than as ice picks. Get used to scraping steel on rock.

The best way to practice "dry tooling" is by bouldering at the bottom of a rock cliff. Falling even a few feet with crampons and tools is dangerous, so stay low. A couple feet off the ground is plenty.

Use the axe and hammer blades like skyhooks. Probe behind bumps, edges, and shelves for any flat place that will hold a tooth or two. Look everywhere. Try everything. Put the pick above a potential hold, then gently slide it down. If it catches, apply more weight until it either pops or stays put. Keep your face clear — wear a helmet just in case — and keep your arm steady. Push down or pull out on the shaft and the pick will skate. A steady downward pull is key.

The ideal dry-tool placements are incut and will hold body weight, although a placement doesn't have to be bomber to be usable. Keep your weight distributed over your feet and the bleakest edge or bump can hold you while that fourth limb searches yet higher. Again, you'll learn how far you can push dry tooling by practicing close to the ground — not on lead.

You'll use the picks largely for hooking, but they work other ways as well. Set them over natural chockstones or ice lumps frozen in the cracks. Torque the blade in thin cracks or constrictions.

No crack? No ice? No hooks? How about planting the tip in a clump of frozen moss or dirt? I've gotten plenty of solid

Barry Blanchard mixing it up along the Ghost River, Alberta.

Anything goes.

organic placements and have even hooked the pick through tree roots on several occasions. Rule nothing out.

Don't forget about the other parts of the tool. Turn the tool around and jam the adze or hammer head in a crack. In horizontal cracks, shove the shaft straight in as deep as it'll go and lever up on it.

When there's no obvious placement, it's time for the "drag and search." Reach as high as you can and drag the pick down the face. If it doesn't catch, move it over an inch and try again. Continue until you've exhausted all possibilities.

That failing, it may be time to go down.

But then, maybe you overlooked something. Look closer. Get mischievous. Moving a tool or crampon a mere inch higher might give you just the height you need to get the next placement.

Do what you must, but don't get sloppy and hack away fragile potential placements. Analyze ice lumps before you blast them apart looking for a rock placement. Even a half-dollar-sized blob can, if it's bonded well to the rock, hold a pick. Before you hit it, study the lump carefully to determine where it's thickest, and strike there. Hit with short, light taps. Pecking disturbs the ice less than rearing back and smacking it. Once you've carved an acceptable niche, set the pick in it and pull down, hooking just as you'd do on a rock edge.

Nothing for the tools? Let them dangle from your wrist loops and use your hands — gloved, mitted, or bare, whatever the situation calls for. Grab small icicles. Palm dihedral and gully walls. Throw fist and hand jams when you can. Use your entire body —knees, butt, back, elbows, head — to friction. Pile and wool clothing grips better than slick shell gear. Consider switching into these higher-friction clothes before you head out.

Crampons on rock

You can't climb snowy or iced-up rock with bare boots, so keep your crampons on and get psyched to use them on rock. The best placements are flat ledges that take several points, but crampons can friction on slopers and seat in the

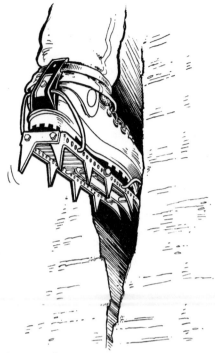
Boot–crampon jam

tiniest divot, even ones that only take a single point.

Work the side points as well as front points. Use the inside points to edge just as you would in rock shoes. Front-pointing gives you more reach, but when possible, I use the side points. They are more stable, and the foot position is less tiring.

Set your crampon on the hold and press. As with the tools, easy does it. A little weight at first, then more. Think of your feet as your belay. Place them well, keep your weight on them, and you can be solid even though your tool placements are shaky.

Tight corners and cracks present new opportunities. Try bridging the crampons crosswise in corners, and if there's a wide crack, jam your boot, crampon and all. In thin cracks, try torquing or jamming a front point.

The above pertains to rock, but don't overlook the meager dollops of ice spattered here and there. Press your crampon points into these, or lightly tap them in. Ice that doesn't completely break away is probably usable. Apply weight and see.

Mixed protection

Your tools are on rock. Your crampons are on rock. Guess where you'll be putting most of the gear? Carry a good selection of pitons, from long knifeblades to a 1-inch angle. Long Leeper-Zs are particularly useful for blasting into iced-up cracks. Bring plenty of tie-offs and a minimum of six over-the-shoulder runners. Toss in a full selection of cams and a handful of wired nuts. Finally, in the event you do find thick ice, carry a couple of short screws and an ice hook or two.

You're racked for El Cap, so make the most of it. Scour the walls for gear placements. Many good placements lie just under the snow — rake it away — or are on the wall

behind you. Don't bypass protection just because the climbing is
easy — it might not be so simple
later on, and, as usually happens,
the protection and holds get
sketchy together.

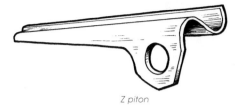

Z piton

Pound in pins. Set screws. Chip the ice out of cracks and
slip in a cam. Use those nuts. Hammer them in if you must.
Chockstones, icicles, flakes, roots, and branches are gifts.
Sling them. Thread holes in the ice. If a hole doesn't go all
the way through, chip it through with your pick. Open your
mind — that's what mixed climbing is all about.

Getting Down

"This is a stupid way to die," I thought, as I slid on all fours toward the edge and a 900-foot drop into the fine Canadian hardwoods.

It had been a long and enjoyable day of bashing ice on the Pomme D'Or, a 1000-foot golden ribbon in Quebec. The sun was out, and the 50 mph winds that had been raging all week were now but a gentle breeze. Great conditions. Kevin Cooney and I made the first rappel off a tree. At the ledge below, Kevin set the screws for the next rap while I dealt with the ropes and slings. I planted both my tools off to one

"How do we get down?" The Gremlin's Cap, Cordillera Sarmiento, Patagonia, Chile.

side and got on my knees to thread the screws. And started sliding. I grabbed for my tools. Couldn't reach them. Grabbed for the ropes. Couldn't reach them, either. I tried to get up on my crampons, but the combination of the icy ledge and my slick shell pants made that impossible.

Then it sank in — I wasn't going to stop sliding, and the drop behind me was forever. I panicked and pawed fruitlessly at the ice. Yep, goner.

But just as I was uncomfortably near the edge, Kevin stepped over, grabbed me by the pants, and pulled me to my feet.

Hallelujah.

Sliding or falling off a belay ledge is just one of numerous ways to get the chop on a rappel descent. You can rap off the ends of the rope. The anchors can pull. Ice or rock can blap you on the head ... you get the picture. There are a thousand ways to die, none of them glamorous. To make sure you survive to see the golden years, here's a quick primer on the anchors and techniques specific to snow and ice. You already know how to rappel, so we'll skip the nuances of sliding down a rope.

Ice anchors

An experienced ice climber and mountaineer can construct solid anchors from the worst pile of rubble. Still, walk off or crampon down an easy slope when you can — no need to tempt fate.

Established routes will likely have fixed rappel stations. Common set-ups are slung trees, bolts, pins, nuts, and screws. All are subject to the mountain's harsh freeze/thaw cycles, degenerating ultraviolet rays, and corroding moisture; test them carefully. Lightly tap pins to make sure they are still tight. Crank on screws to check their placement. Examine everything. Pull the webbing clear of the snow and ice and scope every inch — sometimes runners get cramponed, or dropped, then freeze onto a ledge, giving the appearance of a fixed anchor. Replace any webbing that is worn, or that you just feel weird about using. Also, double up the anchor if it is less than bomber. Don't die because you're cheap.

If you're forging new ground, or got off route and can't find the fixed rappel, you'll have to rig the stations yourself.

Solid rock anchors and sturdy trees should be your first choice. These are generally the most dependable and easiest to rig. Set rock gear as you're already accustomed to doing, but with trees place the rappel sling high on the trunk or around a high, large limb so the rope can clear the cliff edge and run free of deep snow, which can make for hard pulls.

When there are no rock anchors or trees, you'll have to anchor into the ice or snow. Ice screws work great, but at $45 a pop, most climbers leave them only as a last resort, or use their antiquated but still reliable "leaver" screws.

For a time, lengths of inexpensive electrical conduit pounded into the ice, hammer-in style, were popular for rigging ice stations. Lately, conduit has fallen out of favor, replaced by the more reliable and multi-directional "hourglass thread."

To make one of these, take two long screws and place them angled toward each other in the ice. Anchor strength depends on the distance between the screws, hole depth (farther apart and deeper is stronger), and ice quality. Angle the screws so they intersect at the back of their holes, and remove them to leave a V-shaped tunnel. Thread the tunnel with 7mm perlon, using a coathanger or other stiff wire to fish out the end. Tie the perlon with a double fisherman's knot, and you're done. In suspect ice, use two or more tunnels and equalize them.

Other creative and dependable anchors are the icicle thread and bollard. Icicles are fast and easy; simply loop the rope around the icicle. Use long runners if you suspect rope drag will be a problem. Icicle diameter and ice quality will determine the anchor's strength. I hesitate to rappel off any icicle that is smaller around than my leg. Bigger is better, and always make sure the icicle isn't cracked and is stuck solidly to the wall.

Chopping a bollard is hard work, especially when the ice is bulletproof. Ease your load by "improving" existing lumps and stumps. Incut the backs and sides to channel a rope, and you're on your way. As with icicles, gauge a bollard's strength by its diameter and ice quality.

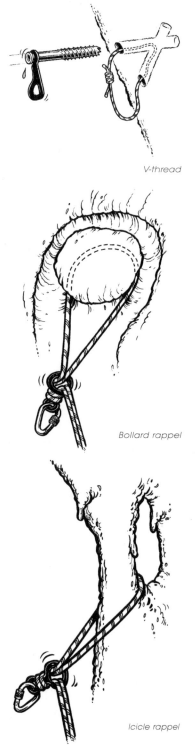

V-thread

Bollard rappel

Icicle rappel

Snow anchors

Bollards, pickets, and flukes are common snow anchors that you can use for rappelling. Bollards are the most time- and labor-intensive, but don't require leaving gear, making them most climbers' first choice. Rig a bollard for rappel the same as you'd do a belay, except, since you'll be pulling the rope, make sure the cord can slide freely around it. You can help it along by lining the bollard with smooth rocks, or, if you have enough runners, sling the bollard and run the rope through the sling. You'll be rapping on the bollard without an axe back-up, so be certain it's bomber.

Pickets and flukes work fine as long as the snow is dense enough to hold them, and as long as you have enough of these things to get down the mountain — unlikely, since most climbers only carry a couple of each at most. Best to master the bollard as a back-up.

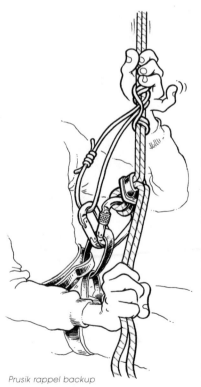

Prusik rappel backup

Getting ready

You are likely rappelling down ice or snow, so keep your crampons on. Have both tools holstered, but at the ready. You'll need the crampons to stay upright and, if the next station is off to one side, the tools to claw your way over to it.

Ice and alpine routes are subject to rock and ice fall, and seemingly insignificant bits of gravel are enough to stun you, causing you to lose control of the rappel. Self-belay with a prusik or ascender on the rope above your rappel device, and use a short tether to attach this to your harness. Hold the prusik or ascender in your top (non-braking) hand, and make sure the tether isn't so long that, should the prusik or ascender engage, it is out of reach.

Take a long runner and use it to anchor yourself at rappel stations, or to your tools while setting an anchor. Girth-hitch the run-

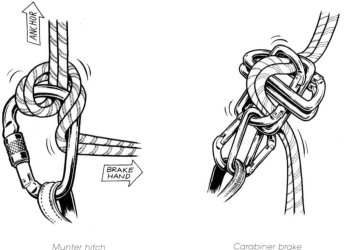

Munter hitch   Carabiner brake

ner to either your rappel/belay loop, or around a leg-loop's crotch strap and the waist belt.

Rappelling frozen ropes

Any rappel device works when your ropes aren't frozen, but when they are, you may have to resort to unorthodox tactics. Try the Munter hitch, or try shoving the ropes into the large hole of your Figure-8, and rappel in Sticht-plate mode. Do not, however, use this last method when the ropes aren't frozen — it doesn't provide enough friction for a controlled descent.

The carabiner-brake is another way to deal with stiff ropes. Two cross carabiners usually will let you move, but if they won't, remove one. Be careful — you're now wholly dependent on one piece of gear.

Still can't budge? You may have to use the Dulfersitz, a traditional and painful technique that works well enough to get you down low-angle faces.

Dulfersitz

Ice is but one of many dangers.

Staying Alive

Michael Kennedy and Greg Child, who collectively can count 20 trips to the Himalaya, had just completed "warming up" on the West Face of Alaska's Mount Huntington, and were taking advantage of a spell of stable weather to attempt the fifth ascent of the difficult *Moonflower Buttress* on nearby Mount Hunter.

Conditions and weather were perfect. Still, eight pitches up, Kennedy had a bad gut feeling that something wasn't right. Nothing was physically wrong, but his intuition told him they should go down. What to do? He weighed his drive for success and his unwillingness to let his partner down against bailing for no logical reason. He relayed his concerns to Child, who, to Kennedy's surprise, agreed that they must heed Kennedy's instincts and rappel.

Who knows what would have happened had they continued? Maybe they would have made it. But maybe the route was primed for avalanche and they would have been swept away. In any event, they returned the following year and established an even more audacious line, spending nine days, including six nights in portaledges, on the *Wall of Shadows* to the left of the *Moonflower*.

Safe climbers heed warnings. These can be as abstract as an uneasy feeling, or as concrete as high clouds accompanied by wind, or recent avalanche activity. Intuitive warnings come from getting in tune with your environment, something no one can teach you. Be alert. The other areas are easier to pin down.

Rock and ice fall

The danger of being hit by rocks or bits of ice cascading from high above is usually limited to mountain or alpine routes, but can also present itself on pillars and flows that have icy or snowy walls, bowls, seracs, or cornices menacing overhead.

Even a seemingly insignificant golf-ball-sized bit of ice or rock can pose a threat. It may not kill you outright, but it can cause you to lose your balance and fall.

Rocks and ice can seemingly fall from nowhere and strike anywhere, but usually you have a few clues. Rocks and fresh chunks of ice imbedded in the slope or at the base of a wall are a bad sign, indicating recent activity. Rapidly rising temperatures can loosen lumps of snow and ice frozen to rock walls, and the resulting meltwater can dislodge stones. Cornices and seracs falling from high above can present significant hazards on some routes.

While the best solution is to avoid areas prone to rock and ice fall, this is sometimes impossible. Travel in these areas early in the morning, when everything is frozen in place, and limit your exposure. For example, zig-zagging up a slope is the least strenuous way to tackle it, but when you suspect that a slope is in the line of fire, run straight up it on front points to minimize your exposure.

Bergschrunds and moats

These are the gaps created by glacial ice pulling away from the rock or ice face. They are essentially crevasses, but ones where one side — the side you must climb onto — is much higher than the other. Problems with "schrunds" and moats are many. First, the walls are usually vertical to overhanging, and the rocky far side can be polished marble-smooth by the scouring glacier. The gap can also seem bottomless, and the span much too far across to bridge.

If the pit is deep, you may have to descend into it, establish a belay, and lead a pitch up the far side. Routine climbing usually, but don't tarry, because moats and schrunds catch the ice and rock set loose by the face overhead.

Avoid schrunds and moats where you can. Traverse up and

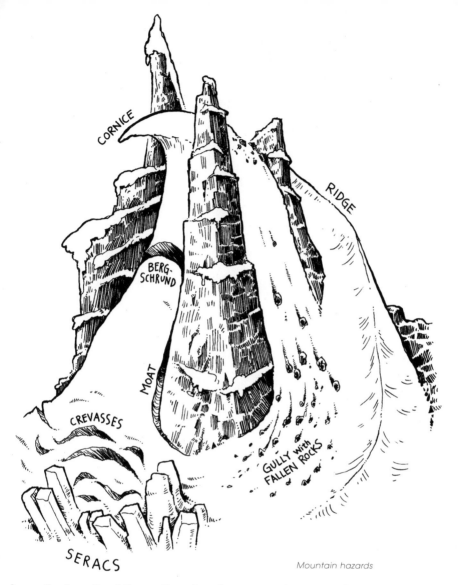

Mountain hazards

down the length of the wall and seek a narrowing spot where you can step, bridge, or leap across. Use discretion for the latter. The route up the wall may not go, and you may not be able to leap back across.

Couloirs

Those striking couloirs that make up many alpine classics also serve as natural catch basins and funnels, collecting stones and debris cast off by the walls above, and rattling the missiles down their narrow throats. And, since couloirs are

Avalanche country.

themselves eroding weaknesses, their walls are typically loose and rotten. Finding good protection in this rock is difficult, as is climbing without knocking rocks on your partner below.

Sticking close to the shelter of the couloir walls, climbing fast, and timing your ascent so you are well clear of the danger zone when the big stuff starts coming down are your best defenses.

Seracs

Seracs, those menacing chunks of glacier that overhang many approaches and sometimes routes themselves, pose a serious danger. The English climber Roger Baxter-Jones was killed while guiding on an alpine trade route, the North Face of the Triolet, when a serac broke from the face above him.

Virtually unaffected by weather and sun, seracs are driven by glacial movement and can collapse without warning any time, day or night, in storm or clear. Stay well clear of seracs and move quickly when you must cross their paths. Also, you might be miles from a serac, but if it falls it can trigger an avalanche when it hits that docile snowslope beneath it.

Cornices

Cornices are another often unseen threat. These mushrooms or brows of snow form due to wind deposition on the leeward side of a ridge. When the weight of the snow accumulation exceeds the cornice's tenacity — something impossible to predict — the whole thing breaks off, sending tons of snow down to pulverize the face below.

It is easy to spot the overhanging curl of a cornice, unless, of course, you are on its windward side, where the cornice will look like the rounded crown of the ridge itself. The danger there is that you will stumble too far over the unseen cornice and plunge right through it. Stay a healthy distance back from the edge.

Timing the climb

Good timing is the most important factor for safely climbing a route. Check with local climbers familiar with the route to determine when rockfall is at its worst. What you'll usually hear is that morning and midday are the most dangerous times. The sun-warmed air, or the radiation of the sun striking the face directly, loosens the ice or snow holding the rubble together. This unmortared debris then succumbs to gravity and comes raining down.

You may have to climb at night when the face is frozen solid and less likely to dump on you. Another bonus of a nighttime raid is that you'll catch snow conditions at their firmest — kicking up firm crust is much preferred to postholing or wallowing in soft snow.

Hike in and bivy near the base during the day. Scope out the route so you're sure of the line — it'll be nearly impossible to get your bearings in the dark — and get a traditional alpine start at around midnight. Do not start up at sunset — the accompanying freezing temperatures create frost wedging, bringing down those loose stones that were on the verge of dropping. Give the face a couple of hours to stabilize, then attack.

Avalanches

As an ice climber you may think that your exposure to avalanches is minimal. It is the snow sloggers and mountaineers who get buried, right?

Hardly. You don't have to be in the backcountry, miles from nowhere, to get buried. Ice forms where it does because those areas are drainages — snow wants to dump down there. And the climb isn't the only danger. Those tame slopes or seemingly mellow snow chutes you have to traverse or climb to get to the ice present very real dangers themselves.

Writing about avalanches is always a sticky wicket because you never quite know how much to put down. Go too far and you'll have a ponderous dissertation. Touch only on the basics and you can give people just enough information to get into trouble.

Numerous fine books already exist on avalanches. Among the best are *Snow Sense* by Fedston and Fesler, and *The Avalanche Handbook* by McClung and Shaerer. Because that literature already exists, and this book is about climbing snow and ice, what follows are the basics. Let these rudiments stick to your ribs, but remember you are not an expert. Get hands-on experience by taking advantage of a multi-day avalanche seminar, and, when you do go in the mountains, go with someone who knows more about avalanches than you.

■ What can slide? Any slope with snow on it is a risk, but slopes with angles between 25 and 60 degrees are the most likely to avalanche; slopes between 35 and 40 degrees are the most dangerous of all. Steeper slopes usually slough off snow as it falls, rather than holding it and then dumping all at once. Lower-angle slopes usually don't stress the snowpack enough for it to slide.

■ When a snowpack loses its grip to the ground slope or the layers of snow under it, it slides. But it doesn't just slide for no reason. Maybe it got heavier because of recent snowfall, and the added weight overcame the snow's tenuous bond. Or maybe the sun caused thermal changes in the snow that broke it down, causing it to cut loose.

Or, most likely, some foolish climber jumped into the snow basin, thus fracturing it, shocking it into release, or adding just enough weight to trigger the slide. Fact is, avalanches occur in the mountains all the time, although the majority of slide victims get caught in avalanches they've triggered themselves.

■ Changes in the weather cause changes in the snowpack, usually for the worse. Rain, wind, snowfall, sunshine, and cloud cover all undermine the integrity of snow.

The most dangerous time is within the 24 hours just after a storm, and the faster the snow accumulation, the greater the chances of avalanche. Use the day or two after a storm passes to get your gear squared away. The time you spend sharpening your tools, cleaning the stove, and rewiring your headlamp may just save your life.

One of the most dangerous times is a period of settled weather, followed by storm. During the sunny days the surface snow will have hardened, making it difficult for the fresh snow to bond with it.

Warming trends increase the moisture content in the snowpack, increasing the avalanche danger. Conversely, storms 25 degrees Fahrenheit and colder don't let the new snow stick well to the old, also increasing the avalanche danger.

You don't usually associate rain with snow, but it happens. Rain warms the snow and makes it more dense, and can cause a lubricating film of water to build between the layers. A poisonous recipe.

■ The best way to survive an avalanche is to stay out of it. Plot your course so you avoid the danger slope, or at the least, minimize your exposure to it. Ask around. Check with the locals to determine the danger areas. Avalanches occur on the same slopes over and over, and people who frequent an area will likely know where those spots are.

Look for clues to tell you about past or possible avalanche activity. Surface cracks indicate the start of a slab avalanche. Trees bent over or with limbs scoured off on one side show that an avalanche has passed here before, and will likely do so again. Convex slopes are more likely to slide than concave ones. Use your ears and listen for the

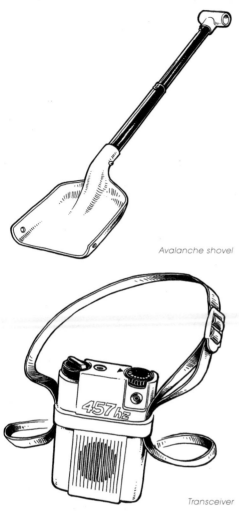

Avalanche shovel

Transceiver

tell-tale "whump" of a weak, collapsing snow layer.

Ridges are safer than open bowls or broad slopes, but watch that you don't stumble over a cornice. Travel on the windward side (the side getting hit by the wind) of a slope, where much of the snow has probably been blasted clear. When you must cross an avalanche slope, climb as high as you can and traverse above the bulk of the snowpack. Cross one at a time and move quickly to minimize your exposure. If you are climbing the slope, cruise straight up instead of zig-zagging, and hug the side. Subsequent members should follow in the same tracks to minimize snow disturbance. Before you take off, zip up your jacket, remove ski or axe straps from your wrists, and loosen pack straps so you can ditch those items if you're caught — you'll be more apt to extract yourself from a slide if you're unencumbered, plus discarded gear will provide clues to the searchers.

■ Ice axes are poor avalanche probes, and your hands make a pitiful shovel. Each climber should, in avalanche country, carry ski poles that telescope into workable probes and a sturdy, broad-bladed shovel. Route difficulties will often prevent carrying those items, but there's never an excuse to travel without an avalanche transceiver. Wear the unit on a cord around your neck. Put in fresh batteries at the beginning of each season, test each transceiver before setting out, and make sure each member of your party is well versed in its use.

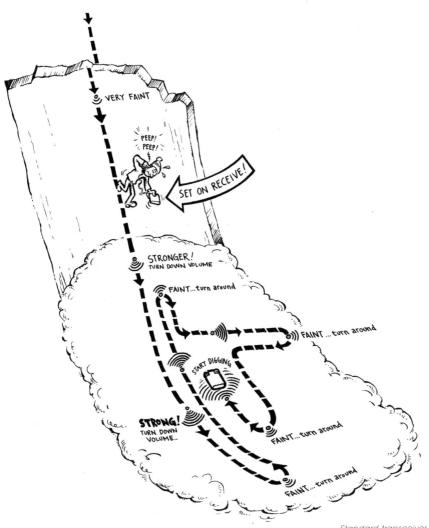

VERY FAINT

PEEP!
PEEP!

SET ON RECEIVE!

STRONGER!
TURN DOWN VOLUME

FAINT...turn around

FAINT...turn around

START DIGGING

STRONG!
TURN DOWN
VOLUME...

FAINT...turn around

FAINT...turn around

Standard transceiver search

■ If you're caught in a slide there's little you can do —
gravity and the mass of the snow will suck you along and
dump you out where they want. Still, try to escape. Brake
with your axe or arms to let the mass of the slide pass under
you. Swim to stay near the surface, and roll or flop to try to
get to one side, where the snow is shallowest. As you feel the
snow slow and begin to settle, make one last effort to free
yourself. Lunge for the surface, then take a deep breath and
use your hands and arms to create an air pocket in front of
your face. Once buried, relax to conserve oxygen. Yelp only
when you are certain someone is near.

What to do if your buddy is buried

Keep your wits. Your friend's life depends on how well you conduct yourself in the next 30 minutes. Do not go for help — there isn't time for that, as few buried avalanche victims survive beyond an hour. Begin the search immediately.

First, consider whether or not the slope might slide again — you won't be any good to your buried friend if you get covered yourself. In a high-risk situation where there's more than one searcher, let only one or two people search, while the others observe from a safe point, ready to spring into action if the searchers get buried.

Note and mark where the victim was last seen, and look for surface clues, such as clothing or gear, to establish a line of travel and track your partner. Switch your transceiver to receive, and make certain everyone in your party does the same.

Work your way methodically down the slope from the last-seen point in a standard transceiver sweep, which will vary according to your brand of transceiver and the terrain and conditions. The accompanying illustration on the previous page shows a generic sweep pattern.

If you were foolish enough to venture out without a transceiver, begin a coarse probe, paying special attention to likely catch points, such as trees, boulders, and depressions. Two or more people should stand five feet apart and probe in front of and on each side of their bodies before advancing a short step downslope and probing again. Dig like mad, but carefully, when the probe strikes a solid object. Search until you find the victim or collapse.

Finally, you can take all the avalanche courses, read until your retinas shrivel, and spend a lifetime studying snowpack, and still die in an avalanche because it was inconvenient not to. You knew the danger was high, but you went out anyway because you didn't travel halfway around the globe, spend your savings, and burn two years' worth of vacation to sit in a tent and wait for stable conditions. Be patient. Having the sense and being willing to avoid dangerous conditions will, more than anything, keep you alive.

Glacier travel

You can climb ice all your life and never get caught in an avalanche or step through a cornice or have a pillar fall from underneath you, but venture onto glaciers and you will fall in a crevasse.

Thankfully, punching into a crevasse doesn't have to be as bad as it sounds. If the rope is kept tight, usually your leg will just jab through the crust, and a move with the ice axe or a pull on the rope is all you need to extract yourself.

It can be much worse, and it can happen to anyone. The very experienced alpinist Mugs Stump died when the lip of a crevasse gave way, and the renowned soloist Rennato Cassarotto was killed when he plunged into a crevasse while returning to basecamp after a nearly successful solo bid on K2.

Avoiding crevasses is the obvious way to stay out of trouble. Plan your trip so you catch bare, snow-free glaciers. You'll find these in the warmer, summer months. Being able to see the crevasses can shave many frustrating hours off the approach and make the going much safer.

Find the path of least resistance before you step on the glacier. Scope the glacier from a high vantage point, and pick a line that weaves through solid ground, usually near the center of the glacier, where there are fewer stress fractures. Glacier edges, particularly where they round a bend, are usually rife with cracks, making the going difficult and tedious.

A rope team of three is ideal, leaving two climbers free to extract and attend to the unfortunate down in the hole. If you have three climbers, have one clip to the middle of the rope with a locking carabiner. The other two should clip to either end. Don't tie in — a knot, especially a wet one that has held a fall, can be impossible to untie, something you'll need to do if one of you falls in.

Three on a rope is ideal, but most alpine teams are teams of two. Not to worry. Two can still safely cross glaciers; they just have to take extra precautions. First, each climber should clip to the rope 60 feet from an end. Coil and sling the

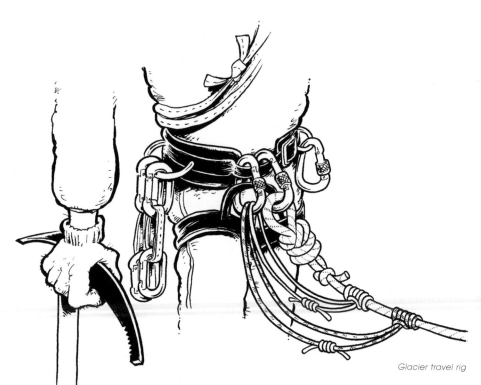

remaining rope over your shoulders. Keep the coiled rope longer than the length of rope binding the two climbers. Make it shorter and you won't be able to toss it in to the fallen climber, who will need it to prusik or jumar out.

Prepare for self-rescue by placing two prusiks, or ascenders, on the rope in front of your clip-in. Clip yourself to each prusik, and have an aider (or long runners that can work as aiders) within easy reach. Now, should you drop in a crevasse, you can jug out with minimal effort.

As you cross the glacier, keep the rope reasonably taut — slack only adds distance to a fall. Don't carry "hand coils" as many books and articles suggest. Hand coils are nothing more than slack. Keep the rope tight and the friction of it knifing into the snow will usually keep the leader from going in over his head, making extraction quick and simple.

Finding a safe path is up to the leader. Experience will give you an eye for detecting pits lurking under the snow. Give depressions and shadowy areas a wide berth. These may indicate holes underneath. Probe vigorously with the axe, or better, a telescoping ski pole with the basket removed. Feel for any changes in resistance that might indicate a crevasse.

You usually needn't stop to belay. Rather, move at a pace that keeps the rope snug and constantly advancing. Stop and set a belay at trouble spots, such as snow bridges, which can collapse without warning.

You've fallen in. How you get out depends on how deep you are, whether or not you are injured, and the nature of the crevasse. In the simplest case, you are only in up to your armpits and can hand-over-hand back up the rope.

Next best, you are in deep but unhurt. Remove your pack and clip it to the rope your partner has tossed in to you. Pull out the aider, clip it to the bottom prusik, and prusik out. You'll probably run into a problem at the lip, where the rope has sawed into the snow. Tunnel through, and use the rope the pack is hanging on for assistance.

Then again, there might be another way out of the crevasse. Can you chimney or front-point up the walls? Or lower to the crevasse floor and walk to a point where you can climb or scramble out?

Worse case, your partner is in the crevasse and is hurt, possibly unconscious. Set pickets, screws, deadmen, or whatever solid anchors you can construct, clip the rope to these using one of your prusiks, and unclip yourself.

Anchor the rope, then uncoil the slack from your shoulders and toss this in next to your partner. To prevent the rope from slicing into the lip of the crevasse, stick your pack under it as a pad. Attach your prusiks to the rope and, thus self-belayed, peek into the crevasse to see what's up. If your partner is unconscious and/or upside down, rappel in on the slack rope and get him upright. Be careful. Make sure you can get yourself back out — there won't be anyone left on top to rescue you if you get stuck.

If your partner is unconscious or hurt and can't get himself out, you are going to have to haul him out. Forget about pulling him up hand-over-hand. You must rig a complicated

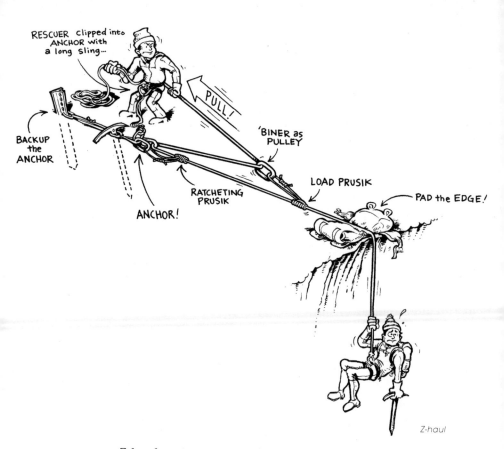

RESCUER clipped into ANCHOR with a long sling...

BACKUP the ANCHOR

PULL!

'BINER as PULLEY

LOAD PRUSIK

PAD the EDGE!

RATCHETING PRUSIK

ANCHOR!

Z-haul

Z-haul system to get the necessary mechanical advantage. Lay the rope out in a Z pattern. Set one prusik or ascender on the rope near the lip, and put the other on the same piece of rope, but just below the anchor. The prusik near the anchor will prevent the rope from back-slipping.

Attach a carabiner, or pulley if you are lucky enough to have one, on the rope between this ascender and the anchor. Clip this biner or pulley to the anchor. Attach another carabiner or pulley to the rope at the other bend in the Z, and use a long runner to clip this to the ascender or prusik at the lip. Make sure everything is set nice and clean, with no tangles or confusing wads. Now, haul on the free arm of the Z. The 2-to-1 mechanical advantage generated by the system will enable you to lift your partner. As you haul, the prusik near the crevasse will advance toward the anchor. Move it back down to the lip long before it can touch the holding prusik, or else the system can snap into a straight line, and you'll have to rig everything all over again.

Your biggest obstacle will be getting your partner over the crevasse lip, where he'll jam into the snow. The best way to get him free is to belay yourself to the lip on a tight rope, grab his harness, and yard him out.

Tea time. Kevin Cooney in Quebec, Canada.

Comfortably Numb

Climbing ice and snow is like playing poker: Know just enough to get in the game, and you are going to get beaten like a mule. To an extent, that is unavoidable and preferred — you'll only grab a hot skillet once. This isn't to say, however, that you should suffer needlessly. Stack the deck when you can. Ergo, a few tips to ease your plight.

Training

Train for ice climbing? You betcha. Getting fit for ice might seem ridiculous, but alpine and mountain climbing is much more physical than rock climbing and the consequences of flaming out and falling are far graver.

Forearms and calves are the first to fail you on a steep ice pitch, so give them the most attention. Consider yourself fit when you can crush walnuts with your bare hands and your flexed calves are so taut that hot needles won't penetrate them. Get them that way at least two months before the season by blasting them with calf raises, wrist curls, and pullups.

Do calf raises by standing with your toes on a book or two-by-four and raising and lowering your ankles until your heel almost touches the floor. You can do these without the elevating book or board, but you won't get the same burn nor will you stretch the muscles as thoroughly. Three sets to failure are plenty, provided you do them five days a week. No slacking.

Wrist curls develop crucial shaft-gripping strength and endurance. The easiest way to do these is to load up a barbell with iron and curl away. Seated wrist curls — your wrists bent over your knees — are the most specific, but can hurt your wrists. A better way is to stand, elbows slightly bent, palms out, and curl the bar until it falls out of your hands. To go for the really deep burn, let the bar roll to your fingertips, then roll it back up into your palms.

One excellent variation is the wrist roller, a device you can make yourself. Saw off 18 inches of broom handle, drill a hole through the middle, thread four feet of perlon through the hole, knot one end, and tie a pile of weights on the other. Use it by holding the handle in front of you and rolling it so the cord winds around the handle, lifting the weight. Once the weight winds all the way to the handle, reverse the roll and slowly lower the weight. Punish yourself. Do these until you cramp, every day of the week.

Pullups you can do on a bar or fingerboard. You do these joy-less exercises already, so I needn't elaborate other than to say that you can do ice-climbing-specific pullups by suspending two lengths of broom handle or PVC pipe, gripping these as you would your ice tools, and pulling away.

Augment the above exercises with a brutal regimen of crunches, pushups, dips, all types of weight lifting, and jogging, and you might be ready for ice. Physically anyway. Mental fitness is another matter, and one equally important. Think about it. I'll bet the last time you flamed out you did so out of fear. You were plenty strong, but the greedy fear leech sucked you dry.

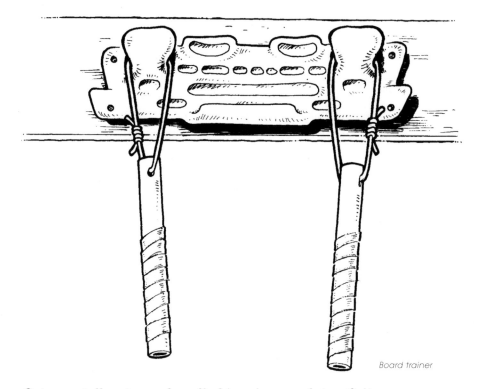

Board trainer

Get mentally strong by climbing ice — lots of it. Familiarity breeds confidence. If you don't have a partner, go ice bouldering. Climb 10 feet up and down a route or traverse its base. Anything you can do to swing a tool will gain you valuable experience, build confidence, and beat back the ugly pump.

Refreshments

Assuage hunger and slake thirst at the first pangs. Deprive yourself of either food or liquids and you'll lose power, seize up, and be a lumbering, babbling burden to your partners. Eat and drink at every opportunity. You'll be happier and peppier for it, and it will also help ward off the cold and keep you mentally sharp.

Gatorade and similar sports drinks are fine on-the-go. Drink two quarts a day, minimum, regardless of how cold it is. When weight or bulk isn't an issue, supplement this with a thermos of hot tea or java. A shot of hot liquids to the gut gets the blood pumping and boosts morale.

Take energy food that requires a minimum of cooking. High-fat foods, such as nuts, salami, dates, Slim Jims, cheese, and energy bars, are ready snacks. Keep them in your pockets, where they'll stay warm, pliable, and easy to reach. The rad alpine boys chow whole cayenne peppers to stimulate circulation, and chase those with shots of olive oil.

Cheating

- Put a shake-and-warm in each mitten and the toe of your boots. These little heaters really work, and they last most of a day.

- Carry several pairs of gloves and mittens: a pair for the approach, where you'll be wallowing in snow and your handwear is sure to get soaked; a dexterous pair for climbing; and a thick, warm pair for belaying.

- Bring one heavy, insulated jacket for two climbers; the belayer wears it at stances.

- Wrap the shaft of your tools with a layer of friction tape to improve the grip.

- Keep your insulated water bottle next to your body where it will be slower to freeze.

- Wear a baseball cap on drippy routes. The bill will shield your face and glasses from the spray.

- Be the first on the ice at popular areas. Many climbers don't get moving until after 10. Beat them and you'll get more done.

- Use a 100-meter 9.5mm rope on long alpine routes. The extra length will let you bypass belays, saving time, and there will be no joining knot to hang up on the rappels.

- Stash an emergency space blanket between your helmet suspension and liner.

- Spray your shell gear with a durable-waterproof-treatment (DWR) a couple of times a season. A fresh application of DWR will improve a leaky waterproof/breathable's water repellency.

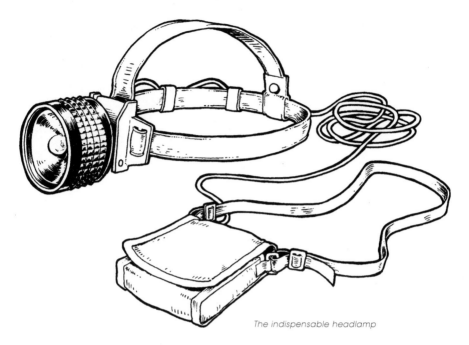

The indispensable headlamp

■ Getting good, safe ice conditions often requires that you hike to the route in the predawn hours. On longer routes, you'll also climb into the night and bivy, or pick your way down and out in the dark. All of these situations require a headlamp. Get a reliable, bright, lightweight, and weather-proof model. Ones with halogen bulbs put out more light, but drain batteries quicker.

Cerro Torre, Patagonia.

Ratings

You, and everyone else who climbs ice, are so confused. You just did a so-called Grade V pillar and it was a stroll — you almost got lulled into a nap at the crux. Then, with a chest full of confidence, you got on an "easier" Grade IV and got the sin gripped out of you. What gives?

Although ice grades can give you a general idea of a route's difficulty, ice rarely forms the same way from season to season. Due to variations in temperature, wind, snowpack, and water volume, a route can be thin and extreme one season, and fat and easy the next. Route difficulty also changes throughout the season. Early on, a drip can be fragile and unprotectable. Come back three months later and it can be a nice big blob, carved into a staircase by numerous ascents. Use a climb's ratings as a dubious guideline and prepare for the worst.

The most common ice ratings are the AI and WI grades. AI designates "alpine ice," those gullies and smears in the high mountains that never or rarely melt. Alpine ice can be neve, hard black ice, water ice that continually melts and reforms, or any combination. Generally, alpine-ice routes are lower angle than frozen waterfall routes, but longer and with higher objective dangers.

Jeff Lowe grappling with Octapussy M8, above Vail, Colorado.

Dan Cauthorn making the grade on Cerro Torre.

WI means "water ice," those seasonal routes formed from frozen seep or waterfalls. Water ice can form cascades, rolling flows, vertical pillars, or smears on walls.

The WI and AI prefixes are followed by a difficulty grade from 1 to 7+. Some guidebooks, like the Canadian *Waterfall Ice*, also tack on a "commitment grade" using the Roman numerals I to VII. This factors in the approach and descent, the route's length and sustained nature, and objective dangers.

The following is a breakdown of the standard WI grades. (For alpine ice, substitute AI for WI.)

WI 1. Low-angle, nearly flat ice like that you'd find on a glacier. You need crampons, but only one tool for occasional balance. Most people walk up Grade I ice and don't even realize it.

WI 2. Still not very steep, but you have to pull on a tool on occasion.

WI 3. Steep enough to require two tools, but you can still usually flat-foot. Grade 3s usually have stretches of Grade 2 ice, with the odd steeper bulge.

WI 4. Beginning to get hard. Near vertical to vertical ice. Grade 4 can be wicked hard in lead conditions, feeling more like 5 or 6. The typical Grade 4 is vertical for 10 to 20 feet, lays back, then gets steep again, then lays back, then ... A vertical pillar can still be a Grade 4, provided it's short — say under a half-rope high.

WI 5. Vertical ice with infrequent resting stations. You are on front points and wrist loops nearly the entire distance. Grade 5s are typically over 80 feet high, but are usually fat and protectable. The *Rigid Designator* in Colorado, *Polar Circus* in the Canadian Rockies, *Repentance* in New Hampshire, and the seldom-formed *Widow's Tears* in Yosemite Valley are all consensus 5s, but they can feel a grade easier or harder, depending on the season and traffic.

WI 6. Free-hanging pillars that are several pitches high, don't touch the ground, or are frightfully slender. Few if any rests and sections of danger. The Canadian Rockies' *Nemesis* and *Curtain Call* are two of the better-known 6s.

WI 7. Nightmares. Tottering, delicate formations that you can blow down with a heady flatulence. 7s are usually rotten, chandeliered, or free-hanging, and require all-stops-pulled-out climbing. Or else they are extremely thin, and your tools punch clear through the ice and hook the nubbins and such on the underlying rock. Spotty pro almost always. The *Sea of Vapors* in the Canadian Rockies is a typical 7: multi-pitched, thin, technical ice, and scarce protection.

Those are the ice grades. Throw in bits of rock climbing and you have to tack on an additional grade. The usual rock-climbing grades of 5.1 and beyond are common, although some climbers lump the ice and rock grades together. They will take a 5.8 WI 5, and, factoring in how much the rock increases the route's difficulty, simply rate it WI 6. Then again, they might use the new open-ended "M" (mixed) grading system, and give it an M5. Or rate using the "NEI" (New England Ice) or one of the Scottish or French systems. Go figure.

Russell Hooper on The Drool, near Redstone, Colorado.

Postscript

"There, it's done," I thought, as I listened to the printer sputter over the final page of this book. "At last I can go climbing."

Then the edited copy came back with a big slash through the ending. It seems I had dwelled too much on the gloom and doom of climbing ice. How the tears well up in your eyes, snot freezes on your lips, and you get all run-out and scared, not knowing if you'll make it. How sometimes it gets so bad you cry out for your mother.

Write something "a bit more positive, like it's really fun to do this stuff," was the comment. "Might as well fool them if we can!"

For several days I tried to patch together a tidy, inspirational ending. I was about done with that when it struck me — there's no need to fool anyone. Being in the mountains, flat-footing up an icefield or front-pointing a hanging pillar, is fun. Up there, you do as you please. There are no bills to worry over. No time clock to punch — other than the one that has you out before sunrise to catch the good ice conditions. No work. No traffic. No politicking. That's why we climb in the mountains.

And if at times the climbing seems like torture, when the spindrift cuts your face or you smash your bloody knuckles against the ice (again), at least it is a bearable torture. You aren't tied to a rack being burnt with embers or flayed with a rusty knife. You can quit any time you like, though I've never met anyone who did. As soon as you get home, those miseries get behind you. Forgotten. The day you settle back into your comfortable life you start charging the walls and staring out windows.

You put up with the grind of work or school as long as you can or is required. But then, one day, the phone rings one too many times, or the line at the gas pumps seems unending. The air smells bad. The food foul. "Enough of this," you cry. You grab your ice tools and are gone. No fooling.

Index

PHOTO CREDITS
Page iv photo by Duane Raleigh
Page 2 photo by Kevin Vessel
Page 5 photo by Duane Raleigh
Page 6 photo by Duane Raleigh
Page 9 photo by Beth Wald
Page 15 photo by Duane Raleigh
Page 16 photo by Dudley Chelton
Page 26 photo by Duane Raleigh
Page 35 photo by James Burwick
Page 38 photo by Cameron Lawson
Page 40 photo by Duane Raleigh
Page 42 photo by Duane Raleigh
Page 50 photo by Duane Raleigh
Page 54 photo by Bill Hatcher
Page 56 photo by Duane Raleigh
Page 60 photo by Duane Raleigh
Page 67 photo by Beth Wald
Page 68 photo by Duane Raleigh
Page 69 photo by Michael Kennedy
Page 74 photo by Rab Anderson
Page 77 photo by Patrick Morrow
Page 78 photo by Patrick Morrow
Page 82 photo by Gordon Wiltse
Page 88 photo by Greg Adams
Page 92 photo by Chris Goplerud
Page 104 photo by Duane Raleigh
Page 110 photo by Ace Kvale
Page 112 photo by Brad Johnson
Page 113 photo by Jon Krakauer
Page 116 photo by Duane Raleigh